ALAN RICHARDSON

Creeds in the Making

*A Short Introduction to the History of
Christian Doctrine*

FORTRESS PRESS   Philadelphia

First Fortress Press Edition 1981

Published in the United Kingdom by SCM Press, London

Second printing 1984

———————

Library of Congress Cataloging in Publication Data

Richardson, Alan, 1905-1975.
  Creeds in the making.

  1. Theology, Doctrinal—History—Early church, ca. 30–
600.   I. Title.
BT25.R52 1981   230′.09′015   81–43073
ISBN 0–8006–1609–X   AACR2

———————

1073D84   Printed in the United States of America   1–1609

CONTENTS

PUBLISHER'S NOTE

Alan Richardson's *Creeds in the Making* was first published in January 1935, and in the United Kingdom it remained in print for nearly forty years and was again issued in 1980. Fortress Press, by arrangement with the SCM Press of London, is delighted again to make the book available to American readers.

There is no other work of comparable scope which presents the early development of the creeds and Christian doctrine to a genera reading public in quite the same way as this work does, with the freshness, charm, and almost timeless quality of writing and judgment so characteristic of its author. We are, then, happy to reissue the book as an introduction for those coming to creeds and doctrine for the first time, and as a fitting memorial to a great modern pastor and teacher. No attempt has been made to update footnotes or references to other literature; books such as Bernhard Lohse, *A Short History of Christian Doctrine* or Hubert Cunliffe-Jones and Benjamin Drewery, editors, *A History of Christian Doctrine,* both published by Fortress Press, will help the interested reader to explore particular issues further.

September 1981

CHAPTER I

CHRISTIANITY is a historical religion. That is to say, it is a religion which bases its whole view of the universe and human destiny upon certain historical happenings. It does not regard all the recorded facts of history as possessing equal significance for its world-view. Some facts it regards as more important than others. There are, as it were, certain key facts, which must be used in the interpretation and evaluation of all other facts. They are of supreme importance for our whole philosophy of life. These facts are the life, character, teaching and death of Jesus Christ, and, above all, his resurrection; to which must be added the existence of the Church of which he has always been the inspiration, and of the experience of God in Christ which Christians have always enjoyed. It is the business of Christian doctrine to interpret these facts; and Christian theology is simply the attempt to state the significance and implications of these historical facts for our ultimate philosophy or attitude towards life.

In quite recent times attempts have been made to treat Christianity as though it were not a historical religion, but a system of ideas or moral precepts, like Confucianism or Platonism. It has been suggested that we can and should distinguish between the religion of Jesus and the religion about Jesus. The truth of Christianity as a system of ideas, it is said, is not dependent upon whether those ideas were first put forward by Jesus or Paul or anyone else; and the religion which Jesus himself taught was not originally based upon any assumptions about Jesus' own nature or divinity. It is claimed that even if the utterly discredited "Christ-myth" school had been right in its contention that Jesus never existed at all, the system of ideas which is called Christianity would remain true; in fact, Christianity without Jesus would be possible. Origins must not be confused with values.

At first sight this view seems attractive because it suggests that all the problems and difficulties raised by the critical study of the Gospels have nothing whatever to do with the truth of Christianity, and that therefore we need no longer be troubled by them. But this solution of the problem is not satisfactory. In the first place, it is the character and life of Jesus which authenticate his teaching about God and man; as we shall see, it is the actual circumstances of the life, death and resurrection of Jesus which guarantee the truth of the "system of ideas" which comprises Christianity and which turn that system of ideas into a living religion. Secondly, such a system of ideas is vastly different from the historical Christian religion, which has always been faith in a person—a personal relation to the God revealed in

Jesus, not a mere intellectual acceptance of certain teaching about God given by Jesus.

Consequently, if we wish to understand the nature of Christian doctrine, we must from the outset recognise that it is concerned with certain historical facts and their signification. The Apostles' Creed, for example, strongly insists upon the historical facts. We cannot ignore such facts, provided that the modern historico-critical study of the New Testament justifies us in believing that they really happened. If Jesus really lived, died and rose again; if in character he displayed a moral excellence which has never been realised either before or after him; if, after his death, his influence was still powerful over the thought and lives of men, then these facts are surely of the utmost significance for our whole view of the nature of God and the purpose of human life. Our philosophy must be wide enough to explain these facts.

The facts about the historical Jesus are therefore the data of theology. Theology is the attempt to explain them, or to explain their significance for human thought and life. The supreme object of the Christian faith is thus the person of Jesus himself; no one theology or system of doctrine must be identified with the Christian religion. Historical Christianity (by which phrase is meant the mainstream of the development of Christian thought from the first century to the twentieth) is consequently not a system of ideas, but an attitude towards a certain historical person; and for this reason it is not possible or desirable for us to attempt to separate the religion of Jesus from the religion about Jesus. For the content of the Gospel is Jesus himself, not a creed or a doctrine or a theory about him. The acceptance of Christianity as our own personal religion is not a mere assent to an intellectual proposition, but the living response of our whole personality to the fact of Jesus. Doctrine is not the Gospel, but only an attempt to explain the significance of the Gospel.

The clear realisation of the essential nature of the Christian religion explains two things. First, it explains why there is always friction between theology and religion. Religious people very often feel that theology leaves a cold, dead abstraction in the place of what was once a warm and living faith; they fear that rationalisation will explain away and dismember; and indeed a good theologian is not necessarily a man of religion. Theology, like any other study, can become dry and academic. But on the other hand religion without theology is like a body without a skeleton : it lacks that which stiffens and steadies it ; it becomes flabby and weak and sentimental. It tends to degenerate into superstition or pleasant day-dreams. We hear a good deal about religion without theology at the present time ; but it is improbable that a religion unpurged by the discipline of theology or hard thinking will possess any real or permanent value. The fact is that religion without theology is as unthinkable and incomplete as theology without religion : the two are as complementary to one another as theory and practice.

In the second place, the realisation that the essence of the Christian religion is belief in a person rather than in a doctrine or system of ideas explains why doctrines must be re-formulated for every generation, and why no particular system of doctrine can ever be final. Every age must make afresh its own interpretation of the central fact of history. That fact remains the same, but our view of its significance changes, develops, deepens and expands. Jesus Christ himself remains the same yesterday, to-day and for ever: the facts of history do not alter; it is our view of his significance which continually needs re-adjustment and re-interpretation in the light of fuller knowledge and deeper experience. We may go further and say that even our views about Jesus may change; biblical science may reveal to us fuller knowledge of his life and teaching; but the fact of Jesus remains—that he lived in a certain way, taught certain things, was crucified under Pontius Pilate, that he was widely believed to have risen from the dead, and that his followers founded a society which has played an enormous part in the subsequent history of the world—these things are indisputable facts which the passage of time cannot alter, and which require interpretation, in our own age as in every other. Hence, the attempt to identify the teaching of Jesus concerning God's Fatherhood and human brotherhood with the content of the Christian religion is not merely unhistorical but is also theologically inadequate; for all down the ages the Christian religion has always implied the recognition that the person of

Jesus and the facts of his life, death and resurrection are the most significant of all historical facts and the key to the interpretation of our universe.

The people of our own generation, especially the younger folk, probably possess less historical knowledge and less historical sense than any previous generation of educated people. We do not nowadays sufficiently respect the value of the study of history. We live under the domination of science, and the scientist does not need to have studied the history of his science in order to become an expert in it. The average student of physical science knows almost nothing of the science of Newton or the pre-Newtonians. Nor is it necessary that he should, since it is possible to make progress in science without first understanding its history. In other words, the results are separable from the history. But this is not the case with philosophy or theology. Results and history cannot thus be distinguished ; we cannot make progress in these spheres of human knowledge without a full understanding of their history. The great philosophical and theological systems of past ages may become inadequate as the expression of the views of later ages, but they are never transcended : men still remain Platonists or Aristotelians, Augustinians or Pelagians, Thomists or Abelardians. We cannot understand the later systems without having first understood the earlier, because philosophical and theological development is much more completely an organic evolution than is the development of scientific thought. We cannot afford to adopt a patronising attitude towards those who formulated the great philosophical and doctrinal systems of earlier ages, even if we cannot rest satisfied with their modes of expression. We cannot avoid the mistakes they made unless we have studied their teachings. Until a generation or two ago men always looked to the past as to a great treasury of wisdom and knowledge ; but the success of modern science and the scientific method has brought about a new attitude towards the past. It has tended to make us conceited and we are led to suppose that we can altogether forget the past and begin again on our own. It comes rather as a surprise to many to find that anyone who lived before the twentieth century " talked sense " in matters of philosophy or religion. Whereas fifty years ago students approached the writings of the Fathers with the utmost reverence and respect, the modern approach is highly critical and, on the whole, sceptical. Such an attitude towards the past is very foolish, and is born of the false " superiority-complex " which pride in our scientific achievements has given to us. The past is our source of vital information ; the writings of the great thinkers of the past are full of instruction and warning for us, and to neglect their wisdom is to open the door to superstition and presumption. Especially is this true in matters relating to the doctrines of the Church, which can only properly be understood by those who have taken the trouble to study their historical background ; criticism of them which is not based upon the necessary historical knowledge is always unintelligent and unhelpful.

All Christian doctrine arises from Christian experience. Doctrines were not invented by a pope or senior bishop deciding that this or that must be believed, or by a council of venerable old men sitting round a table and agreeing to teach a new doctrine. Yet many people to-day seem to believe that the ancient doctrines and traditional formularies of the Church were originally begotten in this way. Such a belief is as old as the fourth century A.D.; even a great scholar like Ambrose, Bishop of Milan, who died in 397, believed that the Apostles' Creed was written by the twelve Apostles who met in conference and each in turn contributed a clause. By Ambrose's day it was confidently asserted which clause had been contributed by each particular Apostle. But, of course, the Creeds were not composed in this way. Every formulation of doctrine was an attempt to embody a living experience, and so to preserve it and communicate it to another generation.

Doctrines were not formulated at all precisely in the first century A.D. Such primitive formulations of doctrine as appeared in the earliest phases of the Church's history were generally in the form of letters written by someone who wished to convey his experience of the new religion to other believers in perhaps quite different parts of the world. Such early efforts to formulate Christian doctrines may be seen, for example, in St Paul's Epistle to the Romans, or in the letter of an unknown Jewish-Christian writer to an equally unknown group of Christians, which is called the

Epistle to the Hebrews. Not all the letters collected in the New Testament were attempts to formulate and to convey doctrines; many of the Epistles are moral exhortations or practical sermons, like the Epistle of James, though, of course, these are of necessity based on certain doctrinal presuppositions. Sometimes the Epistles deal with questions both of belief and of conduct, which had arisen to puzzle the believers in some local church; thus, Paul's converts at Corinth wrote to ask his advice on certain questions such as divorce, re-marriage, the Lord's Supper, or the resurrection of the dead. The First Epistle to the Corinthians, as it stands in our New Testament, is Paul's reply to the questions which they asked him; and it deals with practical questions like those of Church discipline, divorce, and so on, and also with doctrinal questions such as those of the Eucharist or the Resurrection. When in the following century a collection of these treasured Epistles, preserved by various local churches, began to be made, it was found that there was here a very considerable *corpus* of material which laid down the main truths of Christian belief as well as the chief principles of Christian conduct; and, as time passed, the writings of the first disciples came to be more and more highly prized as giving a valuable indication of the basic tenets of Christian doctrine, and of the general direction in which that doctrine might be adequately developed, clarified and elaborated.

We must therefore clearly understand that in its beginnings Christian doctrine developed out of a direct, living experience. The first formulations of doctrine were merely an attempt to tell others about this experience, so that they too might understand and share it. Doctrine was not then a " dry-as-dust " theology, but a valiant attempt to overcome the difficulties of language and to explain the nature of this new religious experience, in order that others might possess and enjoy it. The earliest doctrinal statements were thus missionary apologetic, not intellectual systems of theological speculation. The Apostles aimed at recording facts, not vague speculations. " That which we have seen and heard declare we unto you, that ye also may have fellowship with us." [1]

While Jesus was still present in the flesh with his disciples as their companion and teacher in Galilee, he was undoubtedly felt by them to be someone of outstanding personality, possessing a certain " numinous " quality, which attracted men, but at the same time caused them to *fear* him (in the old religious sense of that word). Mark's Gospel presents to us a Jesus who in the serene power of his impressiveness caused men to be afraid, to " marvel " and to be amazed. " What manner of a man is this ? " is the keynote of the second Gospel. There can be no doubt that before his crucifixion the person of Jesus had always been treated with profound respect, amounting almost to worship, and certainly to wonder, astonishment and awe. It is even recorded that some did actually attempt to worship this unusual Rabbi,[2] whose spoken word was

[1] 1 John i. 3.   [2] *E.g.* Mark v. 6.

always a sufficient guarantee of its own authority and whose hand was always powerful to heal and to restore. Modern New Testament scholarship is tending to make a good deal of the confession of the Messiahship of Jesus by Peter on the road near Cæsarea Philippi [1] as the central feature and turning-point of the earthly career of Jesus.[2] There is no doubt that Jesus was recognised as being in some way different from ordinary men : it is not for me here to attempt to say what this difference was ; but if we are at all inclined to trust the evidence of the Gospels, we may assume that there was some recognition of the " otherness " of Jesus among his contemporaries, whether the latter were disciples, fishermen, peasants, Pharisees or demon-possessed. In fact, the only class of people who seemed to be unable to see this new quality of Jesus' person was that of the ecclesiastical hierarchy, the self-sufficient, self-satisfied Sadducean heads of orthodoxy in Jerusalem ; but an explanation of this phenomenon is not difficult to find if it be true that only the pure in heart see God. This different quality of Jesus' person was recognised not by the sophisticated professors of a narrow ecclesiasticism, the official ornaments of organised religion, but by the child-like and the unpretentious—even though they were plain simple folk, peasants and fishermen, money-lenders and tax-farmers, and similar people of doubtful reputation. " Depart from me, for I am

[1] Mark viii. 27 ff.
[2] *Cf.* Mr T. W. Manson's important book, *The Teaching of Jesus.*

a sinful man," seems to have been the natural
reaction of the plain man in the presence of the
holiness of Jesus.[1]

Thus, even before the crucifixion it is highly
probable that men regarded Jesus as being different
from other men of his day. There was a new,
attractive, yet awe-inspiring quality in his presence;
" the grace of the Lord Jesus " was a precious
memory long cherished by the early Christian
communities. Nevertheless it is hard to see how
the disciples could have made the recollection of
this quality into a universal religion, had their
experience of Jesus ended with the crucifixion of
their leader on Calvary. Even if they could have
made a religion out of the memory of their former
leader, it would have been the retrospective
religion of an example to be copied, not a religion
of present power and victory, such as Christianity
actually at once became. But it is certain that
primitive Christianity was not the religion of a
mere memory, a religion about the past, but the
religion of a present experience and a future hope.
Without a powerful belief in the resurrection there
could have been no Christianity in the form in
which we find it in the Acts and the Epistles.
The preaching of the early Church was essentially
a preaching of the resurrection.

At first the doctrine of the resurrection of Jesus
was the cardinal teaching of Christianity. The
early speeches of Peter and Stephen recorded in
the Acts show us that the first attempts at evan-
gelisation were simply concerned with telling

[1] Luke v. 8.

others the glorious news that Jesus was risen. "With great power gave the apostles witness of the resurrection of the Lord Jesus, and great grace was upon them all." [1]   For the fact of the resurrection set the seal of the divine approval upon the life and teaching of Jesus ; it ratified the belief of the disciples which they had first confessed on the road near Cæsarea Philippi that Jesus was the appointed Messiah of Old Testament prediction and of popular expectation.   For only God could have raised Jesus from the dead, and such a stupendous act of power could only mean that God had visited and redeemed his people. "The God of our fathers raised up Jesus, whom ye slew and hanged on a tree.   Him hath God exalted with his right hand to be a prince and a saviour, for to give repentance to Israel and forgiveness of sins." [2]   The Apostles called themselves simply, " witnesses of the resurrection." [3]

Whether we like it or not, we cannot escape from the fact that historically Christianity was founded upon the belief in the resurrection.   No matter what we ourselves think about the possibility or impossibility of miracle or about the fixity of natural law, it is a plain historical fact that the experience of the resurrection was the beginning of Christianity.   It formed the content of the earliest missionary apologetic.   On it were founded the great doctrines of the Church.   It is not merely the central element in the teaching of Peter and his companions ; it is also the foundation stone of the more elaborate theology of Paul.   " If

[1] Acts iv. 33.   [2] Acts v. 30 f.   [3] Acts iii. 15.

Christ be not raised, your faith is vain," cries Paul with passionate intensity; " but now is Christ risen from the dead and become the first-fruits of them that sleep."[1] "If Christ be not risen, then is our preaching vain, and your faith is also vain. Yea, and we are found false witnesses of God."[2] One of Paul's main doctrines is that of the participation of the individual believer in the resurrection of Christ; it is his great gospel of hope and power, for if we suffer in this world, we are suffering with Christ, and therefore with him we achieve victory and resurrection. Having become participators in his death, we become sharers in his resurrection. " We are in trouble on every side, yet not distressed; we are perplexed, but not in despair; persecuted but not forsaken; cast down but not destroyed; always bearing about in the body the dying of the Lord Jesus, that the life also of Jesus might be made manifest in our body . . . knowing that he who raised up the Lord Jesus shall raise us up also by Jesus."[3] Thus, Paul found that in his own experience and in that of his converts, the resurrection of Jesus was an undeniable fact; and many people since Paul's day have claimed to share this experience. But Paul was not content merely to assert the authority of individual experience in determining belief; he gives us the earliest list of the resurrection-appearances of Jesus which we possess—earlier than the accounts in any of the Gospels: " For I delivered unto you

[1] I Cor. xv. 17, 20.   [2] I Cor. xv. 14 f.
[3] 2 Cor. iv. 8 ff.

first of all that which I also received, how that Christ died for our sins according to the scriptures ; and that he was buried, and that he rose again the third day according to the scriptures : and that he was seen of Cephas (*i.e.* Peter), then of the twelve, after that he was seen of above five hundred brethren at once, of whom the greater part remain unto this present, but some are fallen asleep. After that he was seen of James, then of all the apostles ; and last of all he was seen of me also, as of one born out of due time." [1] Thus, whatever we may think of Paul's evidence or its intrinsic probability, at least it is apparent that Paul is at pains to establish his authorities ; and he claims that he is only preaching " that which he had also received."

We cannot understand the development of Christian doctrine unless we have a clear grasp of the facts which that doctrine was invented to explain. The chief fact which called for explanation was the disciples' experience of the resurrection of Jesus. Without the presupposition of this experience the historical formulations of Christian doctrine are meaningless. Some Christians to-day think that we make too great a fuss about the resurrection ; they say that we ought to be content with taking Jesus as our leader and his life as our pattern, without worrying about what happened to Jesus or about his exact relationship to God or about whether he could or could not work miracles. Now these people are often of the salt of the earth ; but they are nearly

[1] 1 Cor. xv. 3 ff.

always so occupied with good works that they have successfully stifled their desire to know—to know the meaning of their life or whether our universe has a purpose. It is obvious that if in any sense Jesus rose from the dead, our view about the meaning of the universe and the destiny of human life will be vastly altered. Our actual conduct, moreover, will be altered by our belief. The resurrection of Jesus cannot be a matter of little importance or merely an academic question. We cannot agree with those who think that all Christian doctrine is irrelevant to life; it is more than a peculiar form of amusement for those whose minds are so twisted, so removed from the realities of the world, that they have come to like theology. We cannot believe that theology is a waste of time for men and women who are concerned with the urgent business of building not a new heaven but a new earth.

It would be nearer to the truth to say that the belief in the resurrection of Jesus is vitally relevant to-day. Our belief makes and moulds our conduct. If it be true that Jesus rose from the dead, then the universe must be accounted for in such a way as will explain that phenomenon. And if we are living in the kind of universe which alone can account for that phenomenon, then it is clear that certain types of conduct are obligatory for us, while others are equally clearly forbidden. Some will be profitable in the long run, others will be uncreative and detrimental. It might then be more obvious that since the world was of the kind in which the resurrection of Jesus did actually happen, or since reality was constituted in that particular way, the highest well-being of mankind might be attained more effectively by co-operation and disarmament than by class-war or international war. A Christian conception of the universe would then be seen to be of supreme importance, in fact, perhaps even a necessary condition for the realisation of a dynamic and abiding peace. It might appear in our generation as certain as it did to Peter and his fellow-Apostles in theirs, that God had indeed raised up the Lord Jesus to be a Prince and a Saviour, giving to-day repentance to a wider Israel, and forgiveness of sins.

It is the object of this book to explain the doctrines of the Church rather than to attempt to prove that the resurrection happened ; for this is a historical question which must be left to the historians to decide. But it might be useful in the remainder of this chapter to say a few words about the historicity of the resurrection belief with a view to removing certain widespread misapprehensions.

In the first place, a considerable amount of time has been wasted in argument about the mode of the resurrection. Was the resurrection physical or spiritual ? Did the Garden Tomb continue to hold the body of Jesus or was it really found empty ? Believers in the resurrection to-day are divided on this question, and it is foolish for them to waste their time in attacking each other when they both firmly believe in the fact of the resurrection. On the one hand it is argued that it is unnecessary to violate belief in natural law by assuming that the body of Jesus rose from the Tomb : it is enough that after his death he was known to be alive, as we shall be alive after our deaths. On the other side it is asked why the Sadducees did not produce the body of Jesus if it still lay in the Tomb, and thus confute the disciples' preaching of the resurrection. Both views are in their way attractive, yet they cannot both be right. The question is a purely historical one for historians to settle, until metaphysicians have made up their minds about the fixity of natural law. But the main point is that this is, after all, only a secondary question. We must not condemn those who hold a different view from our own. The mode of the resurrection is not so important a question as that of the fact of the resurrection. Although we may hold varying views as to how the resurrection took place, this does not really make any difference to the firmness of our belief in the resurrection.

Secondly, a great deal of time can be wasted in trying to make the different narratives of the resurrection-appearances as they occur in the Gospels and in Paul's first letter to the Corinthians consistent with one another. But such an attempt is, I believe, a mistaken method of handling historical documents : we would not, for instance, assert that a battle never took place just because two ancient historians do not give exactly the same story of the way in which it was fought. If we have acquired an accurate view about how the Gospels came to be written—just like other books and other histories—we shall not expect to find absolute agreement with regard to the details of accounts written at different times and in widely different places. It matters little whether the disciples first had their experience of the Risen Christ in Galilee or in Jerusalem. Acrimonious dispute over such points usually obscures our vision of the real argument for the resurrection.

The most cogent line of reasoning which can be advanced to support the belief in the resurrection is that which starts from the certain fact of the existence of the early Church. Mark's Gospel shows us that right up to the trial and death of Jesus his disciples had failed to understand their Master's teaching that the Messiah must suffer. It had gradually been borne in upon Jesus that the only way left to him by which he could bring his message home to an apathetic generation was to go up to Jerusalem and die for it. His disciples could not understand why he was going to Jerusalem ; they were afraid, but they still dared to hope that Messianic glory awaited them in the Holy City. Hence they could still quarrel about who should be the greatest. Thus it happened that when the crisis came and Jesus was taken into custody, they ran away. They thought that all was over. Yet only a few weeks later we find them actually proving from the Scriptures that the Messiah must suffer—the very teaching which they had been unable to receive from their Master in his lifetime. They now boldly argue the point publicly before the people and before the Sanhedrin. Nothing less than a miracle seems to have taken place in their lives. The cowards who had run away even when the inspiration of Jesus' earthly presence was still with them now came back after the crucifixion of their leader and fearlessly faced the very authorities who had been responsible for Jesus' death. Doubt had given place to certainty; caution and timidity are replaced by boldness and an utter disregard of the consequences; Jesus' teaching about suffering is assimilated and proclaimed. In his lifetime in the flesh Jesus had not accomplished this conversion. Great effects must have great causes, and the miracle of the resurrection is easier to accept than the miracle of unbelief. If we reject the fact of the resurrection, we must account in some other way for the existence of the early Church. No explanation, other than that the resurrection of Jesus actually took place, has ever yet been suggested, which is in any satisfactory way either probable or convincing.

CHAPTER II

WE have seen that the earliest Christian doctrine arose as an attempt to explain the first disciples' experience of the Risen Christ. At first it was very difficult for the disciples who had companied with Jesus among the villages of Galilee and upon the road to Jerusalem to realise that this leader, whose earthly fortunes or hardships they had shared for so long, was now to be regarded as the Messiah of the Jews, ascended to his rightful place of honour in the heavens, and sitting at the right hand of God. Yet the facts had compelled them to accept this view. They believed, of course, in a " geographical " heaven above the starry vault of the sky ; the sky which they saw was the floor of the lowest heaven, on which the angels walked. Consequently, when the author of the Acts tells us that Stephen at his martyrdom saw the heavens opened and Jesus standing at the right hand of God,[1] he was merely expressing the Church's faith in the terminology of his day. Such language seems strange to us, but we must remember that our cosmology is very different from that of the first century, and religious ideas are always dressed in the cosmological imagery of their period. Thus, when the

[1] Acts vii. 56.

early Christian said that Jesus sits at God's right hand, he was only saying in the language of his own generation what a modern theologian is trying to say when he talks about the " cosmic significance " of Jesus Christ. From the very earliest times Jesus was regarded as in some way specially revealing God; if Jesus sits at God's right hand, then God must be of a certain character and have a certain purpose for the world. The statement, crude as it may appear to us with out literalist interpretations, is nothing less than a description of the character of God. The character of the supreme God is in essence similar to the character of Jesus : a monarch will choose a man of his own ideals and temperament to be his right-hand man. God's love will be in no way inferior to the love of Jesus. If this statement be true, then our view of the universe and of human destiny will be profoundly modified.

Yet this is the meaning of the Christian doctrine of the Incarnation even in its earliest forms. The character of God is at least as good as that of Jesus, because in Jesus the character of God is revealed. For Peter and those who had been with Jesus in Galilee and Jerusalem the difficulty was to see how their own humble and rejected leader could ever have been exalted to sit at God's right hand, the position of honour accorded to the Sultan's nearest friend and adviser in an eastern court ; yet their experience compelled them to believe that God had thus exalted Jesus. But now another generation of Christians was coming into the Church, among whom was Paul, whose problem was not that of Peter, but rather its opposite—how could the glorious Son of God who dwelt at the Creator's side in eternal glory have been a village carpenter who ultimately came to a convict's end? The early Church answered this question by reciting the simple story of the Passion—the story of how Jesus came to be crucified. The story itself was sufficient apologetic; it needed no elaboration or rhetorical skill to commend itself; it simply moved to its own conclusion, which could be none other than: " Surely this man was Son of God." [1] There is an increasing recognition among New Testament scholars that the Passion narrative was the earliest connected portion of the Gospel stories to be recited and repeated by the earliest disciples.[2] The story as it stood was an all-powerful missionary apologetic; it answered Peter's question as to how their Galilean friend could so wonderfully have become the ascended, glorified Messiah; it answered Paul's question as to how the reigning Son of God could ever have been a village carpenter who suffered the death penalty along with two robbers. The facts as they occurred were their own authentication; and still to-day there is no stronger Christian apologetic than the simple story of how Jesus died, told without comment by St Mark or St Luke. The early existence of the Passion story in the primitive Church shows us that from the first it was the Church's strongest

[1] Mark xv. 39.
[2] Cf. Dr Vincent Taylor's Formation of the Gospel Tradition, pp. 44-50.

line of appeal. The disciples who were led by
Peter came rapidly to identify the great figure of
the prophecy of the Suffering Servant in Isaiah
with their own friend and master, Jesus ; [1] while
Paul, approaching the question from the other
end, gave a similar explanation. This is what he
says :—

> " Jesus was in the form of God, but thought
> it not robbery to be equal with God ; and he
> made himself of no reputation, and took upon
> himself the form of a servant, and was made in
> the likeness of men ; and being found in fashion
> as a man, he humbled himself, and became
> obedient unto death, even the death of the
> cross. Wherefore God also hath highly exalted
> him, and given him a name which is above
> every name, that at the name of Jesus every
> knee should bow." [2]

Paul is here writing in the language of the first
century, but we can see what he is trying to say.
The ancient world knew of many gods, demi-gods
and human beings who had counted it a prize to
be equal with God ; the novel thing about the
Christian doctrine of the Incarnation is that it
tells of one who was in himself equal with
God, yet had not considered this anything to
boast about, but had rather turned his back upon
any divine prerogative which he might have
claimed, and had not shrunk from a course which

---

[1] *E.g.* Acts viii. 32-35 ; *cp.* iii. 18.
[2] Phil. ii. 6-10.

meant a public execution—even the death of the cross.

Thus, right from the very beginnings of Christianity Jesus was regarded as being in some way the manifestation not only of God's character and love, but also of his power—for it was God's act of power which raised Jesus from the dead. Nevertheless God's power was seen to be a very different thing from what men and women had been accustomed to think of as power. It showed itself most supremely in weakness, and majesty was seen to clothe itself most naturally in humility. The power of God could be splendidly revealed in the weak things of the world.[1] If Jesus was the Son of God, his power showed itself most clearly in that he was strong enough not to come down from the cross.[2] The humility of Jesus made a profound impression in a world in which that virtue was almost unknown.

This revelation of his own nature made by God through the Person of Jesus Christ is the theme of every book in the New Testament. We have not space here to discuss the way in which each of the New Testament writers presents his own personal grasp of the message. Most readers will be to some extent familiar with the standpoint of each writer. We must proceed to our main task of describing how succeeding ages regarded the Person and work of Christ. It is true to say that for about a century after the close of the New Testament period—or until about the end of the second century—there is no new and striking

[1] 1 Cor. i. 27 f. [2] Mark xv. 32.

development of Christological opinion within the
Church. Those Church writers of whom we
have any knowledge seem content to re-state and
to assimilate the message of the New Testament
itself. There were several new developments in
men's thought about Jesus during this period, but
we may venture the generalisation that in so far
as these go beyond the positions reached in the
New Testament—that is, in so far as they possess
real originality—the Church as a whole rejected
them as unsatisfactory. In a word, they were
" heretical."

The word *Hairesis*, heresy, is derived from a
verb which in its middle sense means " to choose,"
and thus comes to be used of those who follow
a particular opinion. Thus, the Book of Acts
speaks of the *Hairesis*, "sect" or "party," of the
Pharisees [1] and that of the Sadducees.[2] The use
of the word was thus in itself not necessarily
derogatory in its New Testament sense. But
later the Church as a whole followed the Pauline
injunction to avoid "parties" within the one
Body, for Christ is not divided.[3] The Church's
faith was one, and the sectarian spirit was not to
be tolerated. The menace of internal conflict is
one of the most serious obstacles to the successful
preaching of the Gospel to the world, and the
early Church soon discovered her need to present
a united front to her hostile environment. Thus
the word *Hairesis* took on an unfavourable
connotation. Individual thinkers or schools of
thought, if allowed too free a scope, could not

[1] Acts xv. 5.   [2] Acts v. 17.   [3] 1 Cor. i. 13.

but damage the unity of the Gospel and thus impair the fellowship of the Gospel. But it was inevitable that individual opinions should give birth to schools of thought in the living and creative process of the development of the Church's theology, in her effort to find an adequate expression of the significance of the Person of Christ. As a matter of fact the Church owes a great deal to heretics. For she was led to develop her theology largely through the pressure which they brought to bear upon her; correct formulations were necessary if men were to see the error of the heretical systems. At a time when converts were pouring into the Church from all sides, with many different religious and philosophical view-points, it was inevitable that " heresies " should appear from time to time. Many heretics, whose opinions the Church had to condemn, were men of saintly character, actuated only by the sincerest desire to promote the true religion of the Lord Jesus. For example, Apollinarius in the fourth century was a saintly and Christ-like scholar and bishop, beloved even by those who had to condemn his view. There were, of course, heretics of a less noble kind, sectarians who wished chiefly to augment their own authority and prestige; but it is true to say that on the whole the greatest heretics—the " heresiarchs "—were honest Christians, zealous for the promotion of a true and reverent Christian theology.

One of the earliest parties or schools of thought within the Church was that of the Ebionites. The word may come from the Hebrew *Ebionim*, "poor men," signifying men who held an impoverished theory. This was a Jewish heresy, held by the successors of the Judaisers who opposed St Paul wherever he went, and who wished to fasten circumcision and other Jewish customs upon all Christians. There was a considerable variety of opinion among the Ebionites of the second century, but they seem usually to have confessed Jesus as Messiah (Christ), though some held that he was only the greatest of the prophets. Some seem to have enjoined a strict observance of the Law, others were less rigorous. Since there was a large number of Jews (mainly of the Dispersion) in the early Church, the presence of a Judaising sect or "heresy" in the second-century Church does not surprise us. Since the Jews had by this time come to regard their monotheism as a badge of their nationality and as a principal difference between their own religion and that of their heathen neighbours, it was quite natural that they should be afraid of worshipping Christ, or confessing his divinity, lest their cherished doctrine of the unity of the Godhead should be endangered. The Ebionites seem to have continued to exist for a long time, since Jerome (died, A.D. 420) speaks of them as though they were still teaching their doctrine in his day.

A more serious heresy against which the Church had to contend was that of Docetism, which may perhaps be rendered into English as "Phantomism." This is a Gentile heresy which made its appearance before the close of the New Testament period.

Those who started from the typical Greek view of God as far removed from and uninterested in the world reasoned that if Jesus was to be identified in any real sense with such a God, he could not really have suffered on the cross, since a perfect God would be incapable of suffering. He could not have felt hungry, angry and so on, since the divine nature is immune from such weaknesses. Indeed, he could not really have had a body at all, since contact with imperfect matter would corrupt the perfection of his divinity. To the Greeks, as Paul had found when he attempted to preach to the philosophers at Athens, the cross was foolishness; this was because they held this conception of the transcendence or remoteness of God. Consequently the Docetists argued that the human Jesus was only a phantom, an appearance : God was acting, as it were, in a rôle designed to inspire and to educate men. His emotions, his sufferings, and even his body itself, could not be real, because God could not suffer or feel emotion or have a body. Of course this view denies the reality of the Incarnation ; it makes the life of Jesus nothing more than one of the old Greek myths about the doings of the gods. But the Docetists were not truly converted ; they had not yet abandoned the old Greek conception of God as remote and too holy to have any dealings with our imperfect world ; they were trying to fit Jesus into their preconceived theory of the nature of God, instead of drawing their idea of God from what they had seen in Jesus. To save their theory they were prepared even to deny the reality of the body of Jesus.

"The blood of Christ was still fresh in Judea," says Jerome, "when his body was said to be a phantom." The Epistles of St John (c. A.D. 100) bear witness to the early existence of the Docetic heresy : " Many deceivers are gone forth into the world, even they that confess not that Jesus Christ cometh in the flesh." [1] The Epistles of St Ignatius of Antioch (c. A.D. 110) are full of attacks on the Docetists : " Jesus suffered truly (really), as also he raised himself truly, not as certain unbelievers say, that he suffered in semblance, as they are themselves mere semblance." [2]

It is worth while to pause for a moment to consider a little more deeply this Greek conception of God, which not only underlies Docetism but which was always reappearing in different forms throughout the whole period of the history of the ancient Church. In two at least of its later forms (which we shall presently consider), namely Gnosticism and Arianism, it nearly extinguished the Christian conception of God altogether. The Greek idea of God may be conveniently summed up in two technical words which are sufficiently important to demand a few words of explanation : these are the words " transcendent " and " impassible." When the Greek said that God was transcendent, he implied that the Supreme Being is too lofty, too holy, too much wrapped up in himself, to have any communications with this world. Since he is perfect, he cannot be in any way associated with this realm of imperfection. He cannot have

[1] 2 John 7 ; cf. also 1 John i. 1-3 ; iv. 1-3.
[2] Ad Smyrn. 2.

created this world, for it was believed that matter was to varying degrees evil or unreal ; and to make the Supreme Being the creator of matter or our world would be to deny his perfection. The result of such a view of God is that the ultimate Deity must be to us unknowable and unreachable ; moreover, our world must have been created by some inferior deity who was but an indifferent artificer. Such a view of God, of course, strikes at the root of the Christian doctrine of Incarnation by denying the possibility of the divine condescension : the God of Greek philosophy cannot be interested in the affairs of men. In fact, he is not God at all in the sense in which the word is usually used ; he is God only for philosophers, not for ordinary men and women. The Greek God is totally unlike the living, active God of the Jews, who created the world, planned its course, ordered the destinies of empires, but yet would condescend to hear the prayer of individuals. The Christian conception of God owed more to the Jews than to the Greeks.

By saying that God was impassible, the Greek was stating a highly philosophical view of God's nature. The phrase strictly means that God is Pure Activity ; he is the centre and source of all activity, the Prime Mover or First Cause. Nothing can act upon God, for he is responsible for all action. It is in this sense that God is impassible : nothing outside him can act upon him, influence him or divert his activity. This conception of God as the source of activity is helpful up to a point ; but beyond this point it becomes a source of endless confusion and error. It is made to imply that God has no "passions," or, as we might put it, emotions or feelings. God cannot suffer pain or feel anger, sympathy or sorrow. Such, of course, is not the Christian conception of God. Nor was it the Jewish view; the God of the Old Testament is a being who feels intensely: he feels indignation, "jealousy," wrath, and so on, as well as the gentler emotions. It is curious to reflect that the Greek excludes these "passions" from God's nature in the interests of his doctrine of God's essential activity, and yet it is the Hebrew God who is, in effect, the God of action, the God who sways history, while the Greek God becomes a mere abstraction, a philosopher's God, who is prevented by his own nature from being active in the world !

We must now return to the actual course of the development of thought about the Person of Christ during the second century. After the Docetists come the Gnostics, who also start from the old Greek or pagan conception of God as transcendent and impassible. The Gnostics are familiar figures in the second and third centuries A.D., and they had almost as many followers as had the orthodox Christians themselves. The leading names are those of Marcion (c. A.D. 140), the son of a bishop of Sinope, Basilides (about the same date), and Valentinus (who came and taught in Rome c. A.D. 150), whose system, says Dr Burkitt, was known all over the Christian Churches from the Euphrates to the Rhône. So widespread and influential did these "heresies" become that there grew up at this time the conception of the " Catholic Church," that is, the main body of Christians as distinct from the " heresies " outside it.   In the earliest times, as in the letters of Ignatius, the word "catholic" in the phrase " the Catholic Church " had simply meant " universal "; but owing to the rise of the heretical bodies, it now came to be used as meaning the orthodox, non-schismatic Church opposed to them.   The word " catholic " now became a title, just as it is to-day in the phrase, " the Roman Catholic Church," though perhaps it never quite dropped its suggestion of universality. To speak of more than one catholic Church would be a contradiction; the modern conception of several churches (or denominations) is entirely foreign to the thought of the first four centuries of Christianity. It is in the above sense of " non-schismatic " or " orthodox " that the word " catholic " appears in the Creeds, not in the sense of " universal "; and the modern Protestant interpretation of it as meaning " universal," the sense adopted by the Reformers, is certainly unhistorical. It is in its historical sense that we shall use the word in the following pages.

Amongst modern scholars there are two schools of thought about the Gnostics. One holds that Gnosticism is an essentially un-Christian and even pre-Christian movement of syncretistic thought, which sought to combine elements from different religions and mythologies, resulting in a curious hotch-potch of more-or-less irreconcilable ideas; thus, the figure of the Soter, or Saviour, of non-Christian systems came to be identified with the

Jesus of the Christian tradition.[1] Other scholars, following Dr Burkitt,[2] hold that Gnosticism is an essentially Christian movement, and that the Gnostics were the first Christian philosophers who attempted to give the Church's faith an intellectual expression in terms of the current metaphysical and cosmological ideas of the second century.

Amongst the latter was the Greek doctrine of the transcendence and impassibility of God, which we have already discussed. Accordingly the Gnostics invent a whole series of " æons," " emanations " or " demiurges," which, as lesser deities, mediate between our world and the supreme God. Jesus becomes the chief of these mediators, offering to men salvation from this world of matter and imperfection. Salvation from the world in the Gnostic systems comes not by faith but by knowledge (hence the name " Gnostic," from the Greek *Gnosis*, knowledge). Popular science, especially astrology, supplied the framework of the Gnostic scheme of salvation : the planets were regarded as the heavenly determiners of human destiny. The Ptolemaic conception of the universe was everywhere received with high regard, as is the " mysterious universe " of Jeans and Eddington to-day. The planets were fixed in their crystal spheres which encircle the earth, just as (to use Dr Burkitt's illustration) the outer layers envelop

[1] This view is expressed, for example, in Dr E. F. Scott's article on Gnosticism in Hastings' *Dictionary of Religion and Ethics*.

[2] *Cf.* his readable book, *The Church and Gnosis*.

the heart of an onion.   Through these spheres the soul must penetrate at death, passing the planet-rulers, on its journey to the home of the divine immortality, far beyond the outermost crystal. The planets were thought of as alive, and on the whole unfriendly to men ; somehow the soul must pass them before it reaches its final home.   The Christ-Redeemer came to earth to bring to men *Gnosis* or knowledge of the passwords (usually foreign gibberish or nonsense syllables) by which the soul could deceive and escape the unfriendly planets.

This scheme of salvation presented an attractive way of escape to the men of the second century, and it gained much through being abreast of the popular science of the day.   It seems fantastic indeed to us moderns, but we know that these were the thought-forms of the ancient world.   Gnosti-cism nearly swallowed up Christianity itself in its attempt to identify the latter with the fashionable cosmological speculations of popular Ptolemaic science.   Christian Fathers like Irenæus (*c.* A.D. 180), who resisted Gnosticism, pointed out that the Greek or Gnostic conception of the transcendence or remoteness of God was quite incompatible with the New Testament doctrine of the Incarna-tion, that the Incarnation of God in Jesus Christ redeemed even the world of matter, and that salvation is not by magical passwords, or correct knowledge, as in the mystery-religions, but by faith, by complete trust in God's love, which alone is powerful to save.

If, as Dr Burkitt contends, the Gnostics were

attempting to set forth the Christian faith in terms
of the popular scientific and philosophical beliefs
of their day, it is not for this reason that they
were rightly condemned by the Church. Their
shortcoming was rather that they had too insecure
a grasp of the substance of the Christian religion.
Every age must attempt to present the challenge
of the Person of Christ in terms which are those
of its own living, dynamic thought-forms. In so
far as they were attempting to do this, the Gnostics were on the right track. A more successful
attempt in this direction was made by the great
Alexandrian thinkers of the close of the second
and the first half of the third centuries. Alexandria,
the great and cultured centre of the eastern Roman
world, was at this time pre-eminently the home
of learning and science in the Empire. She had
had a long and distinguished line of Platonising
philosophers, and was also famous for her men
of science and of medicine. The author of the
Book of Wisdom (in the Apocrypha) had lived
there about 50 B.C. Like his successor Philo, he
was a keen student of the Greek philosophers and
of the Jewish Scriptures. Philo taught in Alexandria his doctrine of the Logos while Jesus worked
in the carpenter's shop at Nazareth. During the
second century A.D. a Christian catechetical school
—that is, a school for the instruction of converts
to Christianity—had been founded in the city;
and under Pantenus this school became famous
about A.D. 180. Little is known about Pantenus,
but three great treatises are still extant of his more
famous successor Clement, who became head of

the school about the year 190. Clement, though not a deep thinker, was a man of great piety, wide reading and classical scholarship. He was a keen student of Plato, Pythagoras, Zeno and Aristotle. He held that in the divine providence philosophy had been given to the Greeks just as the Law had been given to the Hebrews to bring them to Christ. The Christian Platonists of Alexandria are surprisingly modern in their outlook : all knowledge is their province, for it is God's gift. Very different is the attitude of Tertullian, Clement's contemporary in North Africa, who regarded Greek philosophy as a snare of the devil—" the bridal gift of the fallen angels to the daughters of men." Clement attempted to explain the Person of Christ by means of the idea of the Logos : Christ is God's Word, his Reason—the Rational Principle whereby God both made and redeemed the world.

Clement's distinguished pupil, Origen, who succeeded him as head of the Catechetical School early in the third century, had in his youth attended the lectures of the (heathen) Platonic philosopher Ammonius Saccus in Alexandria, and was thus for a time a fellow-pupil of this master with Plotinus, the last great non-Christian thinker of the ancient world and the founder of Neoplatonism. Origen was one of the greatest biblical scholars and commentators that the Church has ever possessed ; his defence of Christianity against the heathen Celsus was the most profound apology yet made for the new religion ; and he earned the universal respect of both Christian and pagan scholars. Porphyry, the disciple and biographer of Plotinus, and a stern critic of Christianity, was constrained to admit that " though Origen lived as a Christian, he thought as a Greek." Origen never shirked a difficulty, but boldly discussed every subject. Some of his more adventurous speculations, such as those on pre-existence and on the Fall, brought him into discredit in an age when the narrower spirit of Tertullian had triumphed over the broad-minded, philosophical attitude of free inquiry which had had Alexandria for its home.

Origen made two important contributions to the doctrine of the Person of Christ. First, he definitely subordinated Christ or the Logos to the Father, relying on such passages as " The Father is greater than I." [1] Yet secondly, he clearly taught that the Son is not a mere created thing ; the Son or Logos of God existed from all eternity with the Father. This is known as his doctrine of the Eternal Generation of the Son. God's nature is eternally to be a Father, and therefore the Son could not have been born at a specific moment in time, but must be eternally Son. He is eternally being begotten by the Father, for the latter is the ultimate ground of all that is, be-getting the Logos and creating the world and finite spirits. It is in this sense that the Son is subordinate to the Father, for whereas the Father is the Supreme Being and ground of all other existents, the reality of the Son is derived from that of the Father.

The question of the relationship of the Son to the

[1] John xiv. 28.

Father, which Origen thus attempted to answer, is the ultimate problem of Christology. How is Jesus related to God? In what sense is Jesus divine? How are we to avoid dualism? If Christ be in any sense divine, or if the worship of Christ by Christians is to be legitimate, are there not two Gods, the Father and the Son? The Alexandrians attempt to answer this question, as we have seen, by identifying Christ with the Logos, the Reason-Principle in God, of Greek philosophy. But this solution does not quite remove the difficulty; it is reasonable so far as it goes, but modern men cannot (as the Greeks did) abstract God's Reason from God, set it up as a being in some sense distinct from God, and then proceed to identify this abstraction with the Person of Christ. Nor did the ancient world rest content with such a solution. After the Arian controversy of the fourth century, the Church tacitly ceased to interpret the Person of Christ by means of the Logos philosophy. It is significant to note that the bishops assembled at the Council of Nicea in 325 omitted the word Logos from their Creed, although it appeared in their model, the creed presented by the venerable Eusebius of Cæsarea for the consideration of the Council. We may note also that in Greek thought the Logos is strictly an impersonal conception; it is not a subordinate personal deity over against the supreme Godhead. If both Father and Son are personal, we are still left asking how we can escape belief in two Gods. As we have seen, Origen answered this question by subordinating the Son to the Father, making the

Father alone the ground of all existence, including that of the Son. In the succeeding years both Catholic and heretic built upon Origen's foundation, and each was anxious to claim the great doctor's authority for his view.

Various heretical attempts were made to solve this question of the relation of Christ to the Father. The Monarchians of the later third century were so called because they were anxious to rebut the charge that Christianity was polytheistic and to assert the unity of the Godhead. There could be only one Supreme Being. There were two types of Monarchians. The first type, a school of thinkers known as Dynamic Monarchians, held that Jesus was a *Dynamis*, a power or emanation of God. They are also called Adoptianists, because they believed that Jesus was a man who happened to be so good that God " adopted " him in a special and perhaps unique sense as his Son. Jesus was such a good man that he was able to reveal completely the character and purposes of God. Many people to-day are attracted by Adoptianism, because they feel that it gives them a view of Jesus which is intellectually respectable.[1] The Church, however, rejected this attractive view on the grounds that it impoverishes the Christian doctrine of God. The New Testament speaks of a God who willed to reveal himself, who was not content to wait until there chanced to live a man who happened to be so good that he could reveal him. God revealed himself in

[1] *Cf.* Mr Middleton Murry's book, *Jesus*, or Frank Lenwood's *Jesus, Lord or Leader ?*

Jesus: it is not merely that man revealed God. On the New Testament view God is so utterly loving that he would not leave his message to chance; he so loved the world that he himself took the initiative and sent his Son to redeem the world. Every book in the New Testament is unanimous on this matter. The question is not whether a man could or would ever be good enough to reveal God, but whether God so loves the world as to wish to reveal himself and thus to redeem mankind. Adoptianism does not know of a God who loves sufficiently to take the initiative in world-salvation. It falls short of the Christian doctrine of God in that it does not tell us of a God who was so loving, so interested in the affairs of men, that he conceived a plan for human salvation, whereby erring men and women could be put back upon the right road which alone leads to their highest well-being and peace. The Christian doctrine of the Person of Christ is in reality a doctrine of God's nature and love. Those who deny the Incarnation are not those who find serious difficulties in the formulations of the faith which attempt to explain exactly how God became man, but those who cannot believe that God is so good as eternally to desire to redeem and save the world. These are the real unbelievers. These are they who do not believe either in or with Jesus. Their feet are already on the slippery slope which logically ends in some form of Humanism. They have begun to relapse into the old Greek or pagan view of a God so far away, so transcendent, that he cannot display real interest in or affection for this world—an ancient doctrine whose modern name is Scientific Humanism. For to make God transcendent and unknowable is to set up man as the sole depository of the values, of our hopes and our noblest ambitions. To believe in the Christian doctrine of Incarnation is not merely to believe in Jesus, but to believe with Jesus that God is love. For such reasons the Church rightly condemned Adoptianism, as when Paul of Samosata, Bishop of Antioch, was deposed by a Council held in that city in the year 268.

The other type of Monarchianism is called Modal Monarchianism because it held that the three Persons of the Trinity are not three separate existences or personalities, but only three modes of the existence of the one divine Personality. It is also called Sabellianism after its most thorough-going exponent. Little is definitely known about Sabellius, who seems to have taught his heresy in Rome at the beginning of the third century. For a long time his views enjoyed widespread popularity. He seems to have held that God has played three rôles in history : at first he was Father-Creator, revealing himself through the Jewish Scriptures ; then he abandoned this rôle and became the Son, revealed as the historical Jesus ; after the Ascension, however, he ceased to play this part, and appeared as the Holy Spirit, in which form he is now to be worshipped. The Trinity is thus not an essential Trinity—that is, there is no threefold essence in the Godhead—but an economic Trinity, a Trinity only for purposes of revelation. Sabellianism is thus sometimes called the doctrine of the Economic Trinity. According to the Modalists, God is therefore really one, and the three Persons of the Father, Son and Holy Spirit are only three modes or aspects of his revelation. The exponents of this theory were nicknamed Patripassians, because they held that the one Father-God suffered in the form of the crucified Jesus.

Of course, this crude theory is unsatisfactory. Christianity teaches that God is eternally Father, that his character is eternally that of Jesus, and that he is the ever-active Spirit, inspiring and guiding his world. He does not change his nature from time to time, as an actor changes his rôle. Sabellianism really denies that Fatherhood, the Christ-like character, and the activity of the Spirit are eternal attributes of the divine essence. But the theory served to call attention to points which badly needed discussion, and put up a " No Thoroughfare " notice before still another line of approach. We must reserve our discussion of the questions which this heresy raises, and particularly the question of the exact relationship of the three Persons in the Godhead, until we have traced further the course of the Church's progressive definition of its theology. We now approach the fourth century, the age of the great Councils. The Councils of bishops which met to determine disputed points of doctrine, and which were truly representative of all the local churches of Christendom, were given the title Œcumenical, or General, when their findings were afterwards agreed by the Church as a whole to be an adequate definition of the Catholic position. The four Œcumenical Councils whose decisions we must now consider are those of Nicea (325), Constantinople (381), Ephesus (431) and Chalcedon (451). These four Councils are held to have expressed in a way that is final the Catholic position with regard to the doctrine of the Person of Christ and the doctrine of the Trinity.

THE DOCTRINE OF THE TRINITY

THE conversion to Christianity of the Emperor Constantine in the year A.D. 312 marked a new phase in the triumphant expansion of the Christian religion. But it ushered in an age in which Christianity, instead of being persecuted, now became fashionable, so that many were baptised, not in sincerity but as a mark of respectability. Consequently the Church was crowded with the half-converted, the socially ambitious and the ill-instructed. The pagan idea of God as utterly impassible and transcendent again made its presence felt among those who called themselves Christians. The form which it now assumed is known as Arianism, after its founder, Arius, who began the controversy which split the Church for half a century. A serious danger threatened the fourth-century Church, although her progress seemed outwardly to be invincible : she was threatened with the loss of her specifically Christian conception of God, through the accommodation of her teaching to the tastes of the pagans who now found themselves within her fold. This was the temptation which the Church rejected when she finally expelled the Arians from her midst. For Arianism represents just such an attempt to paganise the Church's idea of God, and so to make her teaching palatable to the unconverted masses both inside and outside her walls.

Arius was a priest in charge of a church in Alexandria, who about the year 318 quarrelled with his bishop, Alexander, over a sermon preached by the latter on the Divinity of Christ. The quarrel rent the Alexandrian Church, and assumed such serious proportions that by 324 the Emperor Constantine felt it necessary to intervene. He sent Hosius, Bishop of Cordova, to attempt to heal the breach. The mission of Hosius failed, and the Emperor, doubtless acting on the suggestion of Hosius, called an Œcumenical or General Council to meet at Nicea in the following year (325), with a view to ending the controversy. Some three hundred and eighteen bishops from all over the civilised world attended the Council. At this Council the Bishop of Alexandria's deacon, the youthful Athanasius, played such a courageous part in the defence of his superior's orthodoxy that the verdict of the assembled bishops was an uncompromising condemnation of Arianism.

The Arians, holding the pagan view of God as unknowable, impassible, unchangeable and unreachable, could not conceive of the Incarnation of such a being. God could have no direct relationship with the world. Moreover, there could only be one Supreme Being of such a kind, and therefore Christ must be a subordinate, created Deity, a mediator between the unknowable Godhead and the world. The Arian Christ was thus neither properly God nor properly man, but a mean between the two; he was not an Incarnation of God but a creature of God's. Certain consequences follow from the Arian conception of God. First, no Incarnation of God is possible, if God be the God of Greek philosophy, since no man can be the vehicle of that which transcends all human experience. Secondly, revelation becomes impossible, for an unknowable God cannot be revealed: only God can reveal God, and if Christ be a creature, how can he be said to reveal the uncreated? Thirdly, redemption is impossible on the Arian view, because only God can redeem mankind. Christ, being a creature, cannot redeem mankind, as Athanasius was quick to point out, since he too would need a mediator between himself and God. Fourthly, all worship of Christ would be creature-worship and therefore idolatry; and therefore the Church's worship of Christ from Apostolic times would be a contravention of the First Commandment.

Thus, the argument turned on the question as to whether Christ was a creature. The Arians appealed to proof-texts from Scripture, especially the passages in the Epistles of St Paul which seem to make Christ subordinate to the Father[1]; and they claimed the authority of Origen's subordination of Christ to the Father. On the other hand the Catholics appealed to other Scriptural texts which would seem to place Christ in the same category as the Father[2]; and they also claimed

---

[1] *E.g.* 1 Cor. xi. 3; xv. 28; Col. i. 15. *Cf.* Mark x. 18; John xiv. 28; Prov. viii. 22 ff.

[2] *E.g.* John x. 30; xiv. 9; Rom. ix. 5.

the support of Origen by pointing to his doctrine of the Eternal Generation of the Son, which is, of course, incompatible with the view that Christ is a creature.

It is not necessary to trace the course of this devastating controversy through the half-century after the Council of Nicea. The whole world took sides, and the Church was rent in sunder. Court scandal, political intrigues, adulation of the Emperor and many other degrading features appeared before the Arian danger was finally averted. At times it seemed as though the Arians had won the battle. In 359 Hosius of Cordova, who had spent a lifetime in the defence of the Catholic position, was forced to recant his beliefs under torture, though he was now an old man; Athanasius himself was exiled for his faith no less than five times from the bishopric of Alexandria in which he had succeeded Alexander. He died, after having been Bishop for forty-seven years, in 373, before the controversy had finally resulted in the victory of the Catholics. He had never wavered in his opposition to Arianism, despite the hardships to which he was subjected; and it is true to say that he is to a large extent responsible for the survival of Catholic Christianity, at any rate in the East, at a time when the Arian triumph had seemed complete. Arianism was abandoned by the West before it was finally defeated in the East; at last, in 381, a Council of one hundred and fifty Eastern bishops met in Constantinople and definitely rejected the Arian position. Although only Eastern bishops were present at Constanti-

nople, this Council has always been reckoned as
Œcumenical, since its findings were generally
agreed upon throughout Christendom and were
actually ratified by the Œcumenical Council of
Chalcedon in 451. Moreover, the West, under
the leadership of the powerful Roman Church,
which had been the sanctuary of the exiled
Athanasius, had now for some time stood firm
by the Catholic position, which had been so
arduously sponsored by Hilary of Poitiers that he
won for himself the title of " the Athanasius of
the West."

By a series of historical blunders the Creed
which the Council of Constantinople is supposed
to have ratified is known to-day as the Nicene
Creed (which can be found in the Communion
Service of the Book of Common Prayer in sub-
stantially the form which the bishops assembled
at Constantinople must have known). Parts of
this Creed are taken over from the Creed affirmed
by the Council of Nicea in 325, which was designed as a statement of the true or Catholic faith
denied by the Arians. This original Creed of
Nicea was thus an emergency Creed, constructed
clause by clause with much care to serve as an
adequate affirmation of those essentials of Christianity which Arianism denied. When we understand this, much that had previously seemed
obscure in the Creed will assume a new and profound significance. In its present form (the form
of the so-called Nicene Creed in the Church of
England Prayer Book) the original Creed of Nicea
is conflated with some other Creed, probably the

Baptismal Creed of the Church of Jerusalem. The Council of Chalcedon ascribes this longer form to the bishops assembled in Constantinople in 381 ; but, since the minutes of the latter Council have been lost, the exact way in which the so-called Nicene Creed came to be associated with the Council of Constantinople is not clear. It is, however, certain that our " Nicene Creed " did not originate at the Council of Constantinople, for in its present form it is found in a treatise called " Ancoratus," written about A.D. 374 by Epiphanius, Bishop of Salamis in Cyprus, who had been perplexed by doubt but had now found an " anchor " for the soul. It was the Council of Chalcedon in 451 which ratified this Creed and so made it authoritative as one of the three great Creeds of Christendom. If we diligently endeavour to obtain a historical appreciation of the meaning and value of the Creed, by taking note of the circumstances under which it came to be authorised, we gain an insight into its real significance, which those who are loudest in their criticism of the Creed rarely possess.[1]

The clauses of the original Creed of Nicea which were specially included to refute Arianism are :—

" And (we believe) in one Lord Jesus Christ, the Son of God, begotten from the Father, only-begotten, that is, of the essence of the

[1] A useful account of the history and meaning of the Creeds may be found in Dr H. D. A. Major's small book, *The Church's Creeds and the Modern Man.*

Father, God from God, Light from Light, very God from very God, begotten not made (*i.e.* created), of one substance (*homoousios*) with the Father."

Controversy focussed upon the last of these clauses, the celebrated *homoousion* clause, which states that Christ is of the very substance of God in a manner which leaves no room for equivocation. Christ is divine, because his nature or essence is that of God. Even the conservative and cautious bishops at Nicea, who were by no means Arian, objected to this clause because of its novelty, its lack of Scriptural warrant, and the fact that the word *homoousios* (" of the same substance ") had been condemned on account of the possibility of a Modalistic interpretation which Paul of Samosata and other Monarchians had given to it in the previous century. The Arians saw that if this clause were accepted, their position could not be made to harmonise with it. Yet owing to the persistence of Athanasius the clause was not merely accepted by the Council of Nicea, but survived the Arian controversy, and is still found in our " Nicene Creed " which was ratified by the Council of Chalcedon in 451. Its significance lies in the fact that it denies the old Greek or Gnostic conception of God as remote, transcendent, uninterested and unknowable ; for it affirms that God's essence is that of Jesus, and that the presence and substance of God are realisable and knowable through Jesus in his character of love. It affirms that God is not unknowable, but is revealed in his very nature of love in Jesus Christ. The God incarnate in Jesus cannot be the distant, unfriendly Supreme Being of pagan philosophy or modern Humanism.

The Council of Constantinople also condemned the heresy known as Macedonianism, after its principal exponent, Bishop Macedonius, who was deposed from the See of Constantinople in the year 360. Macedonius had applied Arian principles to the Holy Spirit, maintaining that though the Son was equal to the Father in substance and dignity, the Holy Spirit was inferior to both, being a creature. The Church as a whole, however, was not attracted by the rather absurd doctrine that the Spirit of God was not divine. Accordingly the Council proclaimed its belief in " the Holy Spirit . . . who with the Father and the Son together is worshipped and glorified," that is, in the unity of the Godhead of Father, Son and Holy Spirit. The age which followed immediately upon the Council of Constantinople witnessed the final elaboration of the Doctrine of the Trinity. The outstanding theologians who completed this work were the " Cappadocian Fathers " and St Augustine, Bishop of Hippo in North Africa.

The Cappadocian Fathers are St Basil of Cæsarea (died, 379), his brother, St Gregory of Nyssa (died, 394), and their friend, St Gregory of Nazianzum (died, 390). Basil and Gregory Nazianzen had been fellow-students with the Emperor Julian in the University of Athens ; Julian in his short reign (361-63) had attempted to institute a pagan renaissance, but had found that Christianity had too strong a foothold in his empire. It is recorded by Christian historians that on his death-bed he cried, "Thou hast conquered, O Galilean!" Yet Julian seems to have entertained a real respect for Basil and Gregory. The three Cappadocian Fathers were at home in classical culture, and were familiar with the current Neoplatonic school of thought, founded by Plotinus (died, 270) in the previous century. They were also keen students of older doctors like Origen. It was they who gave the final formulation to the Nicene theology, and hence they are sometimes called the Neo-Nicenes. St Augustine, accepting and building upon their position, summed up the Church's thought about the Trinity in his notable work *De Trinitate*, published in 416. The classical statement of the doctrine of the Trinity is, however, to be found in the *Quicunque Vult*, which in its turn seems to rest upon the thought of Augustine. The *Quicunque* is often inaccurately called the Athanasian Creed, and may perhaps originally have been dedicated to Athanasius, in an age when "Athanasian" had become a synonym for "orthodox." This Creed can be found in the Book of Common Prayer immediately after Evening Prayer. We cannot date the *Quicunque* exactly, but it probably appeared first in South Gaul towards the middle of the fifth century—or soon after the death of Augustine, which occurred in 430 when the city of Hippo was being besieged by the Vandals. Nor do we know who its author was ; all we can say of him is that he seems to have made a close study of Augustine's

Trinitarian teaching. The first part of the *Quicunque* deals with the Trinity, the second with the Person of Christ.

Augustine tells us that " some are disturbed when they hear that the Father is God, and the Son is God, and the Holy Spirit is God." [1] Many to-day are equally puzzled by the language of the *Quicunque*. Indeed, understanding of this Creed is impossible unless we have made some effort to ascertain the historical circumstances of its composition. In what sense can it be said that there are three Persons in the Godhead ? Our answer to this question depends upon the view which we take of the meaning of the word " person." Those who formulated the Church's doctrine of the Trinity did not mean by " person " what we mean by it to-day—a separate individual personality. It is often assumed that the Christian doctrine of the Trinity commits us to belief in the Godhead as consisting of three separate personalities, and certainly many churchmen thus interpret the doctrine to-day. Such an interpretation is called the " social doctrine " of the Trinity, because the Godhead is thus held to be a society of persons. It is hard to see how any formulation of this view can logically avoid the charge of Tritheism, despite the eminence of the theologians who still adhere to such a theory.

Taking " person " to mean " personality," the upholders of the " social doctrine " argue that, since God is love, he must always have had an object for his love. Since the world did not

[1] *De Trinitate*, I. v. 5.

exist from everlasting, but was created at a certain moment in time, God must have had another object for his love in the countless æons before this world was made. If there is an eternal Lover, there must be an eternal Beloved, since love without an object is an abstraction. The Son, therefore, must have existed eternally as the object of the Father's love. The ingenuity of this reasoning will doubtless surprise anyone who hears it for the first time, yet it is not exhausted at this point. The argument goes on to assert that eternal love, if it existed between two persons only, would be a selfish thing; but love is social, not selfish, and so the existence of love implies that of a society of at least three persons. Thus, we reach the doctrine of three persons (or personalities) in the Godhead. Since the love of the Father and the Son is not selfish but creative, it follows that the Holy Spirit must eternally proceed from the Father and the Son. Thus it is argued that the Father is the subject and source of love, the Son is the object, and the Holy Spirit is the bond of love.[1]

This argument will probably not appear very convincing to most people nowadays; it will seem to them to be too ingenious. Perhaps the chief objection to it is that if God existed *ab initio* as a society of perfect lovers, he (if we may still speak of three persons in this sense as " he ") could have had no possible motive for the creation of the world, since his love had already its satisfying object.

---

[1] *Cf.*, for example, Gore, *Reconstruction of Belief*, pp. 545 ff., or Bicknell, *Theological Introduction to the Thirty-Nine Articles*, pp. 67 f.

However, the early Church did not thus intend the word " person " to mean " personality " in the modern sense. The Latin word *persona* originally meant a part played in social life, the social function of an individual in society, and then the occupier of such a rôle, part or function. Thus it was used of a rôle in a drama, or of the actor in that rôle (*cf.* the phrase which is still used, *dramatis personæ*). In legal circles the word was widely employed in these senses, and we are therefore not surprised to find that the lawyer Tertullian did much to standardise its theological usage. In the Western Church Tertullian's formula, " One Substance, Three Persons," became the characteristic summary of Trinitarian doctrine.

In the East the Greek word *prosopon* corresponded to the Latin *persona*. But it never became the regular word to denote the Persons of the Trinity as *persona* did in the West, because its use by Sabellius and the Modalists (whom we discussed at the end of the last chapter) had spoiled it through giving it heretical associations. Sabellius had argued that the Father, Son and Holy Spirit were merely temporary manifestations (*prosopa*) of the one divine Essence or Personality ; and this view was rightly rejected, as we saw. Thus in the East another word, *hypostasis*, properly the equivalent of the Latin *substantia* (substance), came to be used for the three Persons of the Godhead, in the same sense as *persona* in the West. A certain verbal confusion naturally ensued when the Cappadocian Fathers began to speak of three *hypostases* (the distinctive phrase of the Neo-Nicene school), in the sense of " three Persons." The phrase finally accepted in the East was, " one substance in three *hypostases*," corresponding to Tertullian's formula, " *Una substantia, tres personæ.*"

The terms *persona* and *hypostasis* stood midway between meaning abstract substance (*substantia*, Greek, *ousia*) and concrete individual being. In English we have no word to express their exact meaning. The modern English word " person " suggests too much the idea of separate individual personalities—an idea not necessarily inherent in the ancient terms *persona* and *hypostasis*; while on the other hand " mode," " aspect " and " manifestation " suggest a Modalist or Sabellian interpretation. The word " Persons " suggests Tritheism; the word " modes " suggests Sabellianism. We need a word which means something between the two, if we would arrive at the ancient meaning of the Trinitarian formularies. Professor Raven says that the terms " ' mode ' or ' aspect,' though on the whole . . . less open to objection (than the modern word person), certainly err on the side of minimising the separateness. We have no term which can express the distinction without a difference, the Trinity in Unity of the Godhead. If we could strip ' person ' of its sense of individuality, or ' aspect ' of its impersonal quality, either would serve." [1]

Thus, we cannot well translate the technical terms *persona* and *hypostasis*, as they occur in the traditional formularies of the Faith, by the words " mode " or " aspect," because they suggest that the three

[1] *The Creator Spirit*, p. 27, footnote.

" Persons " of the Trinity are mere attributes of the Godhead. To say that the character of Jesus is an attribute of God is correct so far as it goes, but it leaves out of account all question of the relation of the historical Jesus or Risen Christ to the Godhead. To say that Fatherhood or the activity of the Spirit are attributes of Deity is again correct as far as the statement goes ; but it says nothing about how these attributes are related to one another or to the historical Jesus. And in any case our use of the term " attributes " must not blind us to the fact that God has been revealed to men as Father, Son and Spirit, and that in some way the realities which these names signify must exist " hypostatically," that is, essentially, in God. If we disregard this, we lapse into Modalism. Sabellius was wrong in thinking that the Father-hood, the Christ-nature and the activity of the Spirit were only temporary rôles played by God, just as an actor might consecutively play the three rôles of Brutus, Hamlet and Othello. Father-hood, Christ-like character and spiritual activity are inherent eternally in the nature of God. God is eternally Father, eternally " of the same substance " as Christ, eternally active as the inspiring Spirit in the world.

We may ask whether God is one person (in the modern, not the ancient, sense) or more than one. It should now be clear that the historical doc-trine of the Trinity does not answer this question. It affirms, of course, that God is in some sense personal—otherwise he could not have been in-carnate in Jesus, and Christ could not be *homo-*

ousios with God, that is, of the same substance as God. The question of the personality of God is one of the most fundamental problems of philosophy, and the historical formulations of the Christian faith give us no detailed answer to it. Nor do they profess to do so, because (despite the misconceptions of many people on this point) they do not purport to solve the riddles of metaphysics, but to provide men and women with a working faith adequate to the doubts and difficulties of everyday life. Their purpose is practical, not theoretical. Moreover, personality is a category about which we know little, and it is only in the last few decades that we have begun to understand the nature and possibilities of human individuality. Personality implies limitation : the self implies the not-self, and infinite personality (a self without a not-self) seems a contradiction in terms. Whether, therefore, we ought not to look for a higher category than personality by which to characterise the Supreme Being becomes a very important question. Yet it is just at this point that we must fail, because personality is the highest category in human experience. We can conceive of nothing higher. Perhaps we should content ourselves with saying that God is supra-personal. It may, however, be objected to this proposition that this again makes God an unknown and unknowable transcendent Being, like the God of Greek philosophy. But the answer to this objection is that by saying that God is supra-personal we do not thereby imply that he is not personal. The fact of the Incarnation is for us conclusive evidence that God is not less than personal. He must exist as Father, Son and Holy Spirit—at least, these are the most adequate characterisations of the divine nature so long as we remain bound by the limitations of human experience. A reverent agnosticism is the only possible attitude of the human mind when faced with ultimate questions about the Supreme Being. All that we need to know for the actual business of practical, everyday living is vouchsafed for us in the assurance of Christianity that God may be adequately worshipped as Father, Son and Spirit; and this faith is enshrined (albeit in the language of a generation long departed) in the traditional formulations of the Trinitarian doctrine.

The historical doctrine of the Trinity commits us therefore to belief in the " hypostatic " existence of Fatherhood, the character of Jesus and the activity of the Holy Spirit within the Godhead. It certainly does not commit us to the view that in God three persons (in the modern sense of personalities) exist. At times the Fathers used language suggestive of this rather crude belief, as when Basil of Cæsarea likened the three Persons to three men, Paul, Silas and Timothy.[1] The Cappadocians sometimes use such language, perhaps, let us hope, merely by way of illustration; but, as R. L. Ottley says,[2] " these writers felt a real difficulty in repelling the charge that they taught Tritheism." St Augustine, who did more to fix the doctrine of the Trinity than any other thinker, does not like the analogy of the three

[1] Epistle 38. Quoted by Raven, *The Creator Spirit*, p. 24.
[2] *The Doctrine of the Incarnation*, p. 365.

men, but uses that of the three principal functions of human consciousness—an analogy which certainly suggests one personality with three modes of functioning.

Professor Raven pleads for a return to the standards of the Older Nicenes, who never suggested analogies implying a doctrine of three personalities within the Godhead. He refers us to an illuminating paragraph of Dr Swete's, in which the attitude of the Nicenes—the very Fathers of orthodoxy—is under discussion: " The Church did not attribute to Him (*i.e.* the Spirit), as the Arians did, a personality separate from the personal life of God. The Holy Spirit is an eternally existing mode of the Being of God, and not a separate centre of consciousness and self-determination; the one God, thinking, willing and acting, in one of His three eternal spheres of thought, volition and activity. The Holy Spirit is not, according to the doctrine of the ancient Church, a Divine Individual, but the indivisible Godhead subsisting and operating in one of the essential relations of His Tripersonal Life. If it was asked, How can these things be? the Church of the fourth century answered that it did not know." [1]

Thus, we must regard the three " Persons " of Father, Son and Holy Spirit as three eternal characters, functions or activities rooted in the one divine essence. God is eternally Father-Creator, his character is eternally that of Jesus Christ, and his function is eternally to be operative, inspiring, guiding, sustaining, immanent in the world. The

[1] *The Holy Spirit in the Ancient Church*, p. 376.

true doctrine of the Trinity unites the two philosophical categories of Activity and Being : it is
a doctrine of the relation of God's activity to his
inner nature. " Such a statement," says Professor
Raven, " is not Sabellianism : for Sabellius held that
the aspects were purely temporary and economic.
But it is less tritheistic than what nowadays passes
for orthodoxy. . . . It is at least in the direction
of recovering the original Nicene emphasis upon
the unity and insisting that the distinction of the
Persons must not be explained on the analogy of
three separate human individuals, that we shall
bring our faith into line with the requirements
of religion. It is the one God, at once transcendent and immanent, eternal and revealed in
and through the universe, who for us men is
uniquely manifested as incarnate in Jesus Christ,
and with whom in our moments of inspiration we
are in communion." [1]

But there are several questions which we have
had to set on one side, which now demand our
attention. What is the relation of the Risen Christ
to God the Father ? What was the relation of the
historical Jesus to the Godhead ? How can Jesus
Christ be both God and Man at the same time ?
In order to understand the historical answer given
by the Church to these important questions we
must now examine the circumstances and the conclusions of the Christological discussions of the
fifth century, considering more particularly the
work of the Œcumenical Councils of Ephesus (431)
and Chalcedon (451).

[1] *The Creator Spirit*, p. 27.

CHAPTER IV

THE DOCTRINE OF THE PERSON OF CHRIST

" WHAT think ye of the Christ ? Whose son is he ? " [1] To this ancient question the Church consistently returned the answer that Christ is Son of God and Son of Man : he is truly God and truly man. Does this statement mean anything to us ? We can at least attempt to see what it meant in the ancient Church. The exact position is this : it is not difficult to maintain either, on the one hand, that Christ is God, or, on the other hand, that Christ is man ; the Docetists, as we have seen, maintained that the human Jesus was just God acting a human rôle for our edification ; the Adoptianists had urged that Jesus was a man who became divine : the real difficulty arises when we try to maintain that Christ is at the same time both divine and human. How can Christ be God and man at once ?

The Church as a whole has always believed that it is important to maintain the doctrine that Christ is both God and man. If we say that Christ is God and not man, then all that was human in the historical Jesus disappears, including his ability to suffer, to feel as we feel, or to experience the limitations of our knowledge, and so on. In fact, Jesus ceases to be our Pattern or Example, because

[1] Matt. xxii. 42.

what was possible for him as God is not necessarily possible for us as men. But there are difficulties also if we say that Christ is man and not God. If Jesus were a man, just as other men are, he would still remain our great Pattern and Example, but our doctrine of God would be impoverished. Many people fail to perceive that this is so, and argue that even if Jesus is a man exactly as other men are, we may still believe in the Father-God of whom he spoke. But it must be pointed out that this God would not be the God of the historical Christian faith, for the Christian religion teaches that God was so good, so interested in the affairs of men, that he himself devised a means of our salvation, and " sent " Jesus for our redemption. The Christian faith knows of a God who was not content to allow humanity to muddle through (if that were possible) to its own salvation. In other words, God himself took the initiative and gave Jesus to our race. Now if Jesus be man and not in any sense God, this would not be true : we could not then believe that God was so loving as to take action by way of incarnation on our behalf. Consequently, if Jesus be not in any sense God, God cannot be in the fullest sense a God of love ; in fact, it becomes proportionately harder for us to believe in the existence of a God of love at all. We must realise how important is the doctrine of the Incarnation for our belief in a God of love.

Thus, the denial of either the divinity or the manhood of Christ implies consequences disastrous to the Christian conception of a Father-God.

Though the Church as a whole has always recognised the importance of retaining the full belief
in both the Godhead and the manhood of Christ,
there have generally been two schools of thought
within her fold, one which lays chief stress on the
divinity, and the other which places emphasis
upon the manhood of Christ. The one is sometimes so keen to emphasise the divine nature of
Christ that it pays mere lip-service to the fact of
his humanity : the other is so jealous of the historical human figure of Jesus that his divine significance is sometimes in danger of being overlooked.
In the ancient Church these two tendencies were
displayed respectively by the rival theological
schools of Alexandria and Antioch. The Alexandrians started from the divinity of Christ, and in
their zeal for this truth tended to minimise Christ's
humanity : the Antiochenes were anxious to stress
the reality of Christ's human nature and so tended
to pass over his divinity. Neither school, of
course, went so far as to deny either the humanity
or the divinity of Jesus, and indeed would have
stoutly repudiated the suggestion that it had done
so. But to the Antiochenes the less guarded statements of the Alexandrians seemed to imply sheer
Docetism—the view (which we discussed in the
second chapter) that the humanity of Jesus was a
mere illusion, an apparition, as it were, designed
for our edification. Similarly the Alexandrians
thought that the Antiochenes were Adoptianists
over again, people who said that Jesus was merely
a good man who was " adopted " by God as
his Son. Most people to-day tend to be either

Alexandrians or Antiochenes, since in endeavouring to stress one aspect of Christ's Person it is so easy to pay only formal lip-service to the other; it is difficult to stress equally both the human and the divine natures in Christ.

We spoke in the preceding chapter of the work of the three Cappadocian Fathers who were responsible for the final formulation of the Nicene theology, and who led up to Augustine's thought upon the subject of the Trinity. While they were at work upon Trinitarian doctrine, Apollinarius, Bishop of Laodicea, moved on to a discussion of the problem of Christology. Though a Syrian by birth, Apollinarius was influenced by Alexandrian rather than by Antiochene ideas about the person of Christ.

Apollinarius was an unambitious, studious character, who had already won a considerable reputation for scholarship during the reign of the pagan Emperor Julian (361-63); when the latter forbade Christians to read or teach the classical literature of Greece and Rome, Apollinarius and his father, a schoolmaster, had attempted the enormous task of providing Christian counterparts of all the classics! Their literary output was very considerable. Apollinarius also undertook a scholarly defence of Christianity against Julian and the Neo-platonist philosopher Porphyry, the disciple of Plotinus. He also wrote against the Arians and other heretics, and produced commentaries on many of the books of the Bible. It is a pity that so little of his work survives. He had been a friend of Athanasius and of the Cappadocian, Basil

of Cæsarea.   Epiphanius writing about 377 speaks
of the shock which the Church received when it
learned that the venerable and scholarly Bishop of
Laodicea had fallen into error.   His heretical views
do not seem to have attracted attention till about
371, and he did not secede from the Church till
375.   He was condemned by various councils,
including the Council of Constantinople, in 381.
In 388 his followers were forbidden to partici-
pate in the worship of the Church.   But Apollinarius was never exiled; he died in 392,
remaining a scholar and writer to the end.   His
position is unique among the heresiarchs in the
respect which he commanded even among his
orthodox opponents.

While the Cappadocians were knocking the nails
into the coffin of Arianism and were developing
the Trinitarian theology, Apollinarius attacked the
central Christological problem: How could Jesus
Christ be God and man at the same time?   He
approached this question, as we have said, from
the Alexandrian standpoint, and developed his
theory in conscious opposition to the Antiochene
school.   He begins with the perfect and complete
divinity of Christ: only God could save the world,
and, if Christ is Saviour, he must be divine.   So
far, of course, Apollinarius is loyal to the Nicene
theology.   But while the Cappadocians were content to leave the question vague as to how Godhead and manhood were united in the Person of
Jesus Christ, Apollinarius tried to specify the
precise mode of the Incarnation.   The Church as
yet had never attempted this task.

Apollinarius accepted St Paul's familiar division of human personality into body, soul and spirit.[1] Thus, for his psychology, spirit is the rational, moral and spiritual faculty of man, his distinctively human element ; soul is the physical life—the faculties which men and animals have in common. He then proceeded to say that in the personality of Christ there is no human spirit ; for the place of spirit in Christ was taken by the Logos : Christ was thus Logos, soul and body.   The Logos of God was, as it were, united to the body and soul of a man ; the Scriptural text upon which he chiefly relied was : " The Word (Logos) was made flesh."[2]   Thus, soul and body in Christ were governed by the divine Logos to which they were united : Christ had no human spirit, or mind, and was therefore completely sinless, since sin has its seat in the higher human faculties.   The Logos is, as it were, living a divine life in human flesh.

Of course, Apollinarianism is not a satisfactory solution of the Christological problem, as the Church as a whole at once perceived, because it does not really hold that the Logos became man. Spirit—the distinctively human part of man which is lacking in animals, our rational, moral and spiritual faculties—was not assumed by the Logos ; and therefore Christ was not a man at all : the Logos had, as it were, assumed an animal soul and body ; but it could not be said that in Christ Godhead and manhood were united, because that which distinguishes a man from the animals was

[1] I Thess. v. 23.   [2] John i. 14.

not present in his personality at all. This theory, attractive at first sight, involves the corollary that the historical Jesus was not human at all! The words of the Nicene Creed, " and was made man," become meaningless on the Apollinarian assumption.

Many people to-day are Apollinarian, though they do not know it. In fact, the view which they think is orthodox is itself Apollinarian. Thus, such statements (common in popular and devotional literature) as " Jesus is God," " Veiled in flesh his Godhead see," and so on, are, unless carefully safeguarded, utterly Apollinarian. Often we fall into Apollinarian error through trying to explain the Incarnation in simple, untheological language, as when, for example, we say that in Jesus we see God living a human life for our enlightenment.

The Church was right in rejecting the theory of Apollinarius. Jesus becomes an inexplicable enigma unless he is in the fullest sense human. But the Church did not state her own theory of the mode of the Incarnation, as Apollinarius had bravely done. The exact manner in which Godhead and manhood were united in Jesus Christ was left undefined. The next attempt at more precise definition came from the Antiochene side and is associated with the name of Nestorius. The latter was a monk of the monastery of Euprepius near Antioch, who won such fame for his austerity and eloquence that he became Bishop of Constantinople in A.D. 428. Nestorius seems to have been a well-meaning but tactless person, and he at once became unpopular at Constantinople through his attack upon various heresies, real or supposed. His Antiochene bias is seen in his attack upon the cult of devotion to the Virgin Mary : his chaplain, Anastasius, who had come with him from Antioch, had preached against the title *Theotokos* (which means " Mother of God," " God-bearer ") as applied to the Virgin ; and Nestorius at once championed his subordinate's view. God alone, he urged, could be said to be *Theotokos* : the term, if applied to Mary, might lead lay folk to suppose that Mary was mother of the divine nature of Christ, whereas she was mother only in respect of his human nature. The term might be thought to imply that he who was born of Mary was not man but God, which he felt to be Apollinarian heresy. He therefore suggested the title *Christotokos*, " Mother of Christ." Later in his life Nestorius seems to have modified his view that the term *Theotokos* was fundamentally heretical ; perhaps he had realised his mistake in thinking that the term had not been used by the older Fathers. But the word now became the focus-point of the controversy, just as the term *homoousion* had been a century earlier.

St Cyril, Bishop of Alexandria, now took an interest in the dispute and sent protestations to Rome concerning the utterances of Nestorius. He championed the Alexandrian Christology against the humanising tendencies of the school of Antioch. But Cyril is not a lovable figure ; his motives in attacking Nestorius are not above suspicion, since he wished to exalt the See of Alexandria at the expense of its great rival in the East, Constantinople. He desired to become the "pope" of the Eastern Churches. Nor were his methods above reproach. But he was an astute and capable theologian, and he played an important part in the formulation of the Church's Christological doctrine.

Such serious dimensions did the dispute assume that the Emperor at last agreed to Nestorius' request that a General Council should be called. In 431 the Council of Ephesus, commonly called the Third Œcumenical Council of the Church, met to discuss the matter. Cyril took advantage of the late arrival of the delegates from Antioch and secured Nestorius' condemnation without difficulty. Nestorius naturally refused to appear at such a gathering of his enemies; and when his supporters, the Antiochene bishops, eventually arrived, they held a rival council and condemned Cyril. The Emperor then passed sentence of deposition upon both Cyril and Nestorius; but he later restored Cyril to his archbishopric, while Nestorius was made the scapegoat and sent into exile. He appears to have lived in the Egyptian desert until his death, about the year 450.

The discovery of certain Syrian translations of the actual writings of Nestorius early in the present century has made it highly probable that Nestorius was not personally responsible for the heresy for which he was condemned and which has been named after him. He has been the victim of words, and, we may add, of his own sharp temper. But it now seems clear that he did not believe in what came to be called Nestorianism. The sense in which technical words were used was not yet fixed, and Nestorius was misunderstood by those who used technical terms in a different sense. In the circles in which Cyril of Alexandria wrote it had become customary to speak of the two natures (divine and human) in the one Person of Christ. Nestorius used a word for " nature " which the Alexandrians now used only for " person " in the sense of the Person of Christ. When, therefore, he intended to speak of the two natures or aspects of Christ (divine and human), he was understood to mean that Christ was two persons. His followers, who claimed him as their leader, taught that in Christ a man and God were joined together without inter- mingling, so that Christ was really two persons, a divine and a human. Thus originated Nes- torianism. It was held that there were thus two Sons, the divine and the human persons in Christ, and that there was no real union but only a kind of mechanical conjunction between the two. Superficially, of course, this doctrine of the Two Sons (the Son of God and the Son of Man) who coalesced, as it were, to form the Christ, possesses a certain attraction, and it gained considerable popularity in the Eastern Church. It seemed to solve the knotty problem of how the one person, Jesus Christ, could both suffer as man and yet as God be incapable of suffering. One could say, for example, that it was as Son of God that Christ healed the sick or walked on the water, but as

Son of Man that he wept or confessed his ignorance. (Many people nowadays seem to look upon Christ as though he thus lived in two compartments; they picture him alternately as God or as man, according to their mood or the particular way in which they are thinking about him. By so doing they miss the greatness of the truth that Godhead and manhood have somehow been brought together in the one Person of the Christ.)

Although it is possible for many people thus uncritically to hold a kind of Nestorian view about the person of Jesus Christ, such a doctrine does not bear close scrutiny; and thoughtful folk will not be satisfied with such an impossible view. The Church was undoubtedly right in condemning Nestorianism, even if she was wrong in fathering the theory upon poor, maligned Nestorius. No real Incarnation is effected in the juxtaposition of a divine and a human person in Christ; and nothing is gained by denying that Christ is one person. Ever after the rise of Nestorianism the Church has rightly stressed the unity of Christ's personality. The Incarnation, if it took place at all, must have been a union of God and man within the one incarnate Person of Jesus Christ. The Church was doubtless wrong in attributing this error to Nestorius himself, but Nestorius by his tactless behaviour, his old-fashioned terminology and unguarded statements, was to a large extent responsible for the mistake. He represented an extreme Antiochene point of view, which he expressed in provocative language:

thus, when he attacked the *Theotokos*, or said:
" I could not give the name God to one who was
two or three months old," he was right in so far
as he was opposing Apollinarianism, but wrong
in that he might be understood to mean that the
Incarnation of God in a human child was an impossibility. Nestorianism was condemned again
at the Council of Chalcedon in 451, and the
Nestorians who were expelled from the Church
established the Nestorian Syrian Churches of the
Middle and Far East, some of which survive to
this day.

The necessity of some definition of the Church's
accepted doctrine of the Person of Christ was
becoming more and more obvious, since lack of
official definition was allowing individuals to
formulate and teach their own " heresies," and
thus to stir up strife and promulgate error. The
Church was finally stirred to action after the dis-
graceful affair of Eutychianism had again spread
controversy throughout the East. When Cyril
of Alexandria died, in 444, he was succeeded in
that bishopric by one Dioscorus, who, in order to
set himself up as the head of the Church in the
East, tried to pick a quarrel with Flavian, Bishop
of Constantinople. He therefore supported
Eutyches, an elderly and unlearned monk from a
monastery near Constantinople, who had begun
to teach a kind of Apollinarian Christology.

Eutyches approached the problem of Christology
from an extreme Alexandrian standpoint, and
claimed to be a disciple of Cyril. He fell into the
pit which Cyril had barely managed to avoid, for

he held that the human nature in Christ became swallowed up in the divine. It was transmuted into the divine nature, so that the very body of our Lord was no longer of the same essence as ours, but was a divine body. Thus, he urged that Christ was of two natures before the Incarnation, but only one after it. Flavian's Synod at Constantinople in 448 at once realised that this view was Docetism masquerading in a new guise, and that the distinction between the divine and human natures in Christ must be preserved if a real Incarnation was to be maintained; accordingly the Synod condemned Eutyches, after patiently attempting to explain to him the error of his view.

Henceforward another controversy raged, and the Emperor called a Synod at Ephesus in 449 over which Dioscorus, backed by a large party of Egyptian monks, presided. Violence was used, and the supporters of Flavian were forced to sign a document against their will. Flavian was deposed and died shortly afterwards, as the result (it was said) of injuries which he received at the Council. The whole Church was shocked; and the Bishop of Rome, Leo (the Great), excommunicated Dioscorus and called the Council "the Robber Synod." As soon as a new Emperor came to the throne, in 450, a new Council was called to meet at Chalcedon in the following year. This, the fourth and greatest of the Œcumenical Councils of the Church, ratified the Creeds of Nicea and Constantinople and the work of the Council of Ephesus in 431, condemned Apollinarianism, Nestorianism and

Eutychianism, and produced the important Christological statement known as the Chalcedonian Definition of the Faith, which has become the criterion of the Church's doctrine of the Person of Christ.

Those who to-day criticise the ancient Church for desiring to make creeds and precise formulations of the Church's living faith should reflect upon the circumstances in which these definitions were produced. The Church made no creeds and definitions until these were rendered absolutely necessary for the very existence of the one faith by the false speculations of the heretics. And even when the formulations were undertaken, they were usually drawn up with a view to excluding heretical views rather than with the intention of limiting men's freedom of thought upon the mysteries of the Christian faith. Not until the Arians had attempted to make Christ a kind of demi-god had the doctrine of the Trinity been defined ; not until Apollinarianism, Nestorianism and Eutychianism had run their course was the Church's Christological faith defined. And even after the Chalcedonian Definition was formulated, a good deal of latitude in interpretation was allowed; Alexandrian and Antiochene tendencies were still possible within the limits of orthodoxy.

Thus the Definition of the Faith of the Council of Chalcedon in 451 (which has remained the classic statement of the doctrine of the Person of Christ in the Catholic Church) is mainly negative in its expression. It condemns root and branch the heresies of Apollinarius, Nestorianism and Eutyches, but it does not give reasons why these views are rejected : it merely refers to the arguments of certain letters written by St Cyril of Alexandria and Pope Leo, which it accepts as orthodox statements of the Christian faith. It even asserts that the (revised) Nicene Creed contains all that is essential for belief, and remarks that had it not been for the false interpretations of this Creed by the heretics, no further statement would have been necessary. Finally, it adds a more positive statement of the Church's faith, but even this is formulated with a view to the exclusion of heresy. " We confess (it runs) one and the same Son, our Lord Jesus Christ, perfect in Godhead, perfect in Manhood, truly God and truly man, of a rational soul (anti-Apollinarian) and a body, of one substance with the Father with respect to the Godhead (anti-Arian), and of one substance with us in respect of the Manhood (anti-Eutychian), like us in everything except sin ; begotten of the Father before the ages according to his Godhead (anti-Arian), but in these last days begotten of the Virgin Mary, the God-bearer (*Theotokos*) according to his Manhood (anti-Nestorian), for our sake and for the sake of our salvation ; one and the same Christ, Son, Lord, only-begotten, confessed in two natures unconfusedly, unchangeably (anti-Eutychian), indivisibly, inseparably (anti-Nestorian) ; the distinction of the natures being in no way destroyed through their union (anti-Eutychian), but rather the peculiar quality of each nature being preserved and concurring in one Person and one Substance, not being parted and divided into two persons (anti-Nestorian), but one and the same Son and only-begotten God, the Word, the Lord Jesus Christ."

This passage represents the Church's positive corporate doctrine of the Person of Christ. As we have tried to show by the words in brackets, most of its clauses are directly aimed at controverting heretical ideas. It is therefore obviously un-reasonable to complain, as some people do to-day, that the Church prescribes a rigid and narrow system of closely defined dogma about the Person of Jesus Christ. It is evident that the Chalcedonian Fathers were not attempting to preclude further discussion and investigation of the Church's faith, but were, on the contrary, concerned with removing the false limitations of the subject in the one-sided theories of the heretics. It was the heretics who were one-sided, not the Chalcedonians: it was the heretics who emphasised one aspect to the ex-clusion of the other, whereas the Catholic bishops merely insisted that both aspects should be given full and equal consideration. Thus the Chalce-donian Definition does not prescribe a theory of how Godhead and manhood were united in the one Christ, but contents itself with insisting that they actually were united—a fact which each of the three main types of heresy had denied. The Chalcedonians stand for equal emphasis on both the Godhead and the manhood in Christ as against the heretical emphasis of the one to the exclusion of the other. Thus the Definition stands for a principle rather than for a theory; and it permits the formulation of theories provided that the principle is safeguarded in them. We are free to suggest any theory about the mode of the Incarnation which commends itself to us, provided that we do not lose sight of the fundamental truth that God and man are brought together in the Person of Jesus Christ. The Definition provides us with the postulates or data of Christological theory : it does not attempt to give us a theory of its own. This is the reason why the Definition may remain for those who accept the fundamental claim of the Church—that God himself is incarnate in Jesus Christ—the classic expression of Christological truth ; had the Chalcedonian Fathers attempted to formulate a theory, their work would by now be out of date, for theories must be altered by each generation as the bounds of our knowledge extend. But because they were content merely to enunciate a principle, the Chalcedonians handed down to all succeeding ages a standard by which every theory might be tested and judged.

It is in this sense, and this sense only, that the Chalcedonian formula may be said to be " final." It lays down the principle which must be incorporated in any theory which claims to be consistent with the Catholic faith. Other theories may be constructed, but they will not be Catholic, because they do not agree with the central conclusion of the Catholic Church about the Person of Jesus Christ. Thus the theories of Arius, Apollinarius, the Nestorians or Eutyches did not allow that Jesus Christ was truly God and truly man. We may or we may not accept the conclusion of the Catholic Church about the Person of Jesus ; but

at least we cannot wrangle about what that conclusion is, for the Chalcedonian bishops defined it
unmistakably in the language of their day. This
is the value of the Chalcedonian Definition of the
Faith.

This view, of course, is not incompatible with the
conviction that we must always attempt to set
forth the principle embodied in the Definition in
the terminology and thought-forms of our own
generation. Each generation needs to express old
truth in its own language. But this is equally true
about the message of the Nicene Creed or of the
New Testament itself. It is surely obvious to us
now that the ancient formulations of the faith can
only be understood in the light of painstaking
historical study and research; and it therefore
becomes more and more evident that we need to
restate the ancient faith in modern language in
order that the men of our generation may com-
prehend its message, no longer obscured by the
mists and misconceptions engendered by forgotten
modes of expression. When we have perceived
that the principle enshrined in the Chalcedonian
Definition or the Nicene Creed is the principle for
which the New Testament writers pleaded—that
in the man Jesus Christ we may see the Incarnation
of God—we will realise that we also are confronted
with the same question which these ancients faced
and answered; and at least we shall not let that
question go unanswered because we have not
grasped what it is. We shall then be able honestly
to face the question, " What think ye of Christ? "
and shall the better be able to answer it because we

have considered both the answer which historical Christianity has given and also the answers which have been rejected.

In the remainder of this chapter we shall consider the faith of Chalcedon in the light of modern knowledge and experience, with a view to seeing how that faith may best be explained to the men and women of our own generation. We may perhaps best do this by making three criticisms of the way in which the ancient Church approached the problems of Christology. These criticisms relate not so much to the conclusions at which the ancients arrived as to the postulates or assumptions from which they started and the terminology in which they are set forth. In each line of criticism we may find a constructive suggestion as to the way in which progress in understanding the great doctrines of the Church may be made to-day, owing to the wider outlook and fuller knowledge of our own times.

The first and most obvious criticism of the Chalcedonian theologians arises from the fact that they were inclined to set too great a gulf between God and man. They tended to conceive of God and man as two substances differing from each other in kind and having no properties in common. Of course we can now see that this tendency of their thought was principally due to the accommodation of their thinking to the current philosophy of their day. We have already discussed, in Chapter II, the influence of the old Greek or pagan idea of a transcendent, perfect and far-away Deity, which underlay such heresies as Docetism and

Arianism; the Catholic theologians must be given the credit for having rejected this common view of the Godhead as incompatible with the Christian revelation of God. As we saw, the Supreme Being, on this view, is too remote and too holy to have any dealings with our world of imperfection, and consequently the incarnation of such a God would be unthinkable. Although the Catholic theologians rejected the Greek view of God, it may perhaps be reasonably urged that they did not go far enough. If a real incarnation has taken place at all, this means that God and man cannot be absolutely dissimilar in essence, since they have been brought together in the one Person of Jesus Christ. Wholly dissimilar substances can never be brought together in such a way that a real, organic union is effected. That is why the Arians were forced to deny the Incarnation by making the Son a creature : they had already removed God so far from man. If God was incarnate in Jesus Christ, there must be that in man which is fundamentally capable of being united with Deity.

Thus, in tending to look upon God and man as two different substances, distinct in kind, the Chalcedonians made the problem of an incarnation more difficult than it really is. If there is a great abyss between God and man, a doctrine of incarnation will be hard put to it to bridge it satisfactorily ; but if, on the other hand, God and man are fundamentally akin, as is surely implied by the belief that man was made in the image of God, then the problem as to how God may be incarnate in human life ceases to be an insoluble puzzle. The doctrine of the Incarnation then is seen to mean that God is very near to man, not far away, as the Greeks supposed. If we may admit that perfect humanity is nothing less than Deity incarnate, then it is obvious that our difficulty is beginning to disappear. If we may say that Jesus Christ was truly God because he was perfect man, then we are within sight of a solution to the problem. Yet this is just what seems to many people to be implicit in the Church's teaching that Jesus Christ is truly God and truly man : it is possible for one person to be both divine and human because God incarnate is human nature perfected.

But at this point it is necessary to issue a warning. We must not forthwith proceed to confuse humanity with divinity, for this would be very loose thinking. Humanity remains human, and God does not cease to be divine, even though we admit that man is the image of God, or that Godhead and manhood are not two utterly distinct substances. Even though Jesus Christ be God and man, God remains God and we are still men. The Chalcedonians were right in recognising that there is a distinction between Godhead and manhood, even if they were wrong in tending to suppose that it was a distinction in substance or kind. There is all the difference between man and God that exists between the finite and the infinite, the temporal and the eternal, and, above all, the sinful and the holy. There is all the distinction that exists between the created and the Creator. The appreciation of this distinction lies at the base

of all worship. To surrender, or even to minimise, this distinction would be loss, not gain; it
would be to surrender the essence of religion, as
well as to rob the Incarnation of all significance.
While God and man must not be thought of as
utterly disparate substances, as Arianism and Nestorianism presuppose, they must not be confused
with each other, as Eutychianism confused them
in the Person of Jesus Christ.

Thus we realise that it is permissible for us to
simplify the problem of the Chalcedonians by
recognising that they exaggerated (under the influence of the widespread Greek view of God as
remote) the disparity which exists between God
and man. A second line of constructive criticism
of the Chalcedonian approach to the problem of
Christology is contained in the recognition of the
weakness of ancient psychology. The ancients
possessed an inadequate view of man's nature.
This defect appears most clearly in the illustrations
which the Fathers used concerning the human
nature of Christ. They would commonly refer to
Christ's walking on the water or his miracles of
healing as manifestations of his divine nature; and
they would proceed to mention his feelings of
hunger, thirst or anger, or his physical sufferings,
as marks of his human nature. What immediately
strikes the modern mind is that these latter things
are not distinctively the characteristics of human
nature at all, but of animal nature. Being hungry
or thirsty, feeling anger or pain, are not character-
istically human, for they are experiences shared
with the animal world in general. In fact the

ancients, in speaking of human nature, were inclined to omit altogether what was distinctively human, as apart from the merely animal; this tendency is illustrated by their frequent use of the word "flesh" to signify the manhood of Jesus. We cannot but feel that such a psychology is profoundly mistaken. It tends to place too lowly an estimate upon human nature; it ignores man's achievements, his quest for beauty, truth and righteousness, his longings for the eternal and his capacity for fellowship with God. These things also are human, and our estimate of human nature should be based not upon the qualities which we share with the sub-human world but upon these more distinctively human characteristics. Man is an amphibious creature, capable of living in two worlds, the spiritual as well as the material; he should not be spoken of as a denizen of the lower order only. It was customary among the Fathers to contrast the eternal and unchanging splendour of God with the mortality, changeableness and weakness of men.[1]

This inadequate conception of human nature is, of course, part and parcel of the distinction which the Chalcedonians made between God and man. It renders more difficult the conception of Incarnation, since it removes the human farther from the divine. It tends to turn the problem of Christology into the wholly artificial question as to how God can be incarnate in animal nature. Indeed, it comes very near to Apollinarian heresy, for

[1] *Cf.* Hodgson in *Essays on the Trinity and Incarnation*, ed. Rawlinson, p. 368.

Apollinarius had said that the Logos or Reason of God had been united in the Person of Jesus Christ with the animal body without the human soul. Of course the Chalcedonians explicity condemned the Apollinarian heresy, but it would appear that they had not recognised all that was implicit in the condemnation of that view. Hence, by pursuing this second line of criticism the problem of Christology becomes less difficult for us than it was for the ancients. And in making such a criticism we are being in the fullest sense loyal to Chalcedonian standards, since we are only insisting that Jesus Christ is God and man—perfect man, man most fully human, not merely animal, as Apollinarius had declared.

The third helpful criticism which we may legitimately make of the Chalcedonian formularies concerns their use of impersonal categories instead of living, personal ones. Thus, such words as "substance," "essence," "nature," "*hypostasis*," and so on, are cold, impersonal terms by means of which it is difficult to convey truth concerning the dynamic, living organism which we call personality. Such words are of the language of things rather than of persons. But, as we have noted all along, the ancient theologians were sorely handicapped by the limitations of the languages in which they wrote. As we have had occasion to point out above, the Greek and Latin tongues had no word for "personality" in the sense in which we use that word to-day. Indeed, it was Christian theology which discovered the fact of personality and its significance. But how much more difficult it is to explain such a concretely personal matter as the Incarnation in terms of substances and natures ! It is not easy to explain how God the Father is related to Jesus Christ so long as we are limited to speaking of this relationship as a relationship of substances ; but as soon as we realise that it is a relationship between persons, after the analogy of ordinary human persons, we are able to see more clearly. We do not, of course, understand personal relationships even on the human level, but at least we have direct experience of such relationships in our own lives every day. The unity that exists between two human persons, the actual interflow of two personalities by means of friendship or devotion to a common ideal, remains a mystery for our intellect ; but the unity which is thus attained, the breakdown of all the barriers which divide self from self, is (or can be) a matter of our own experiencing. We have learned nowadays that personalities are not self-contained, impermeable things, and that they overflow beyond the limits of the self, and overlap, as it were, with other selves. This interpenetration of personality becomes more complete as each self grows towards the ideal ; the barriers which divide persons from one another are broken down, and the defences which exclude other selves are swept away. When St Paul speaks of " Christ in me," or when St John speaks of " abiding in Christ," each is speaking of an interpenetration of personality with person- ality which has its analogies on the purely human level and in our everyday experience. If such interpenetration be possible already at the present

stage of human development, with all our incom-
pleteness, selfishness and defence-mechanisms, we
must conclude that on the divine level, where
personality is perfected or perhaps transcended,
complete interpenetration or "one-ness" must be
consummated.

In this practical way we are led dimly to conceive of how God may be incarnate in human life,
how the divine personality may interpenetrate
human selves. We may also partially understand
how God may be incarnate in the human Jesus,
whose personality was thus completely at one (as
all the New Testament evidence proclaims) with
the personality of his Father. God and man
may thus be brought together in the person of
Jesus Christ. No longer need we struggle with
the idea of combining two impersonal substances
or natures, for now we may use fully personal
terms, which are more nearly adequate to the
situation.

It is along such lines as these that the essential
truth which is enshrined in the Definition of
Chalcedon and the other classical formulations of
the faith may be understood and interpreted to-day.
Such reinterpretation of the ancient faith is at once
legitimate and necessary, in order that twentieth-
century people may grasp the truth that indwells
the formularies which they find so difficult to
understand. Of course we must always be on
our guard not to read new meanings of a doubtful kind into the old formularies, for this would
be to put new wine into the old bottles, and
the consequences would be unfortunate. But,

as Dr Inge has somewhere said, there is no
Scriptural injunction against putting the old wine
into new bottles, and this is the ask to which
we must address ourselves to-day, if we wish to
commend the historical Christian religion to our
contemporaries.

CHAPTER V

THE DOCTRINE OF THE ATONEMENT

ALL the classical literature and formulations of the Christian religion, from the New Testament to the Chalcedonian Definition, regard Christ as Redeemer or Saviour. They set forth the belief that by his life and death Jesus brought to men salvation from death and made atonement for their sins. They unanimously teach that in him we find two things—forgiveness of sin and eternal life. Throughout the New Testament Christ's death is connected with these gifts; each writer develops the idea in his own way, but all share the same fundamental standpoint: " Blessed be the Lord God of Israel, for he hath visited and redeemed his people." [1] The Nicene Creed emphasises that it was " for us men and for our salvation " that God became incarnate in Jesus Christ and was made man. So too the *Quicunque Vult* says that it was " for our salvation " that Christ suffered. Likewise the Definition of the Council of Chalcedon says that Jesus Christ was born " in these last days . . . for us and for our salvation."

It is clear, therefore, that concerning this principle the classical statements of the Christian faith are unanimous : that God became incarnate in the

[1] Luke i. 68.

Person of Jesus Christ "for our salvation." This was the sole purpose of the Incarnation. "God sent forth his Son, born of a woman, born under the law, that he might redeem those who were under the law, that we might receive the adoption of sons," says St Paul.[1] "God so loved the world," says the author of the Fourth Gospel, "that he gave his only-begotten Son, that whosoever believeth on him should not perish, but have eternal life."[2] The Fathers also unanimously share the same opinion: St Irenæus, writing at the end of the second century, gave beautiful expression to their view when he said: "The Word of God became man, in order that thou also mayest learn from man how man becomes God."[3]

Throughout the first five centuries of the Christian era the Church was content to assert this principle—that God was incarnate for the sake of our salvation—without elaborating theories as to the exact method by which that salvation was accomplished. Many individuals attempted to think out the mode in which atonement had been made, but the Church as a whole embraced no theory. In this period the situation is exactly as it was in the matter of the Incarnation-doctrine: a principle is enjoined, but no exact theory is affirmed. Again we owe a debt of gratitude to the Fathers who in their wisdom were content to state principles and to refrain from making theories, especially in view of the fact that the attempts at theorising which individual thinkers of

[1] Gal. iv. 4 f.   [2] John iii. 16.   [3] Protrept. i. 8.

this period put forward are crude and unsatisfactory from the point of view of the twentieth century. The New Testament, the Creeds and the Chalcedonian Definition all insist upon the great principle that God in Christ has redeemed man, but there is nowhere in them a hint of theory.

The men of the first five centuries often thought in pictures, and their representation of the Atonement is dramatic rather than intellectual. They thought of Christ as triumphing over hostile " powers," defeating the terrors which men feared —sin, death and the devil. God, as it were, fought a decisive battle with the forces of evil and was victorious. Henceforward the terrors of sin, death and the devil have no further power over men. Such pictorial representation of the principle of salvation conveyed truth in a graphic way to simple minds. But the picture of God fighting with the devil is apt to suggest to modern minds more questions than it answers ; it may express the truth metaphorically, but the modern mind does not accept poetry as a substitute for logical exposition. Indeed, many of the ancients were not content with pictures and resorted to theories. The chief weakness of the picture as seen by modern eyes lies in the dualistic nature of the background against which it is painted : whence came into God's universe these hostile, evil powers, which it was necessary for God to defeat ?

Dr Gustaf Aulén, in his book *Christus Victor*, has called this ancient dramatic view the " classic idea " of the Atonement. It represents God as triumphing in Christ over the tyrants to which man was subject, sin, death and the devil, and as achieving salvation for man, reconciling the world unto himself. The "classic idea" of the Atonement represents, as we have said, not a theory but a poetic representation of theological truth. It is not so much an explanation of the mode of the Atonement as a graphic portrayal of the fact of Atonement. It represents Christ as *Christus Victor* and *Christus Regnans*—as Conqueror and King. His victory is achieved, his work accomplished. Men share in his victory and enjoy the fruits of his work : for us he lived and suffered, conquered and rose again. He procured for us forgiveness of sins and eternal life. The hymns which all the Churches sing at Eastertide show us that the "classic idea" still lives on, and that twentieth-century folk still appreciate the pictorial representation of our salvation.

We have tried all along to make it clear that Christian doctrine always arises from Christian experience. The doctrine of the Atonement is no exception to this rule. All Atonement doctrines, whether ancient or modern, arise from the Christian experience of forgiveness and liberation in and through Jesus Christ. That experience is prior to all doctrinal formulations which express it and to all theories which attempt to explain it. The principle which is laid down in the classical statements of the Christian faith—that God became incarnate in Jesus Christ for the sake of our salvation—is the meaning, intellectually expressed, of the experience of forgiveness and at-one-ment with God which the Church discovered through Jesus Christ her Lord. Since early times men have attempted to explain this principle by means of theories about the fact of the Atonement, in which they have attempted to explain the exact mode of salvation. But we must remember that the Church as a whole is committed to no theory, but only to the great principle which underlies the Christian experience of forgiveness. So long as we safeguard the principle, we are in fact free to construct our own theory, if we wish to do so, without in any sense being disloyal to the historical teaching of the Church. Many different theories about the Atonement have, as we shall see, been held at different periods of the evolution of the Church's theology.

Sooner or later, of course, it was inevitable that theorising should begin. Christians naturally began to ask such questions as : How can the death of Christ render possible the forgiveness of sins ? How does Christ's death bring salvation and eternal life to men ? From what are we saved ? Did God purpose that Christ should die ? Did God suffer in the death of Christ ? When men began trying to formulate answers to such questions as these, various theories of the Atonement arose. We will consider four main types of theory which have actually become prominent during certain periods of the development of the Church's theology. There are, of course, other types of theory than the four which we shall discuss ; but in order that we may understand something of the history of the doctrine of the

Atonement with a view to ascertaining the truth which it contains, it will be well to consider in order the Ransom Theory, the Satisfaction Theory, the Penal Theory and the Moral Theory.

By the end of the second century A.D. there were current many different attitudes towards the redemptive aspect of Christ's life. Some Christian thinkers, like Clement of Alexandria (died *c*. A.D. 214), aiming at *Gnosis* or Knowledge as the ideal of the good life, paid little regard to the fact of sin and the necessity of redemption. Others like Irenæus (*c*. A.D. 180), were interested in developing Paul's mystical view of the summing up of all things in Christ. It was Origen (*c*. A.D. 183-253), Clement's distinguished pupil and successor as head of the school of Alexandria, who first gave expression—almost, we may say, accidentally—to the Ransom Theory, the view that the death of Christ was a ransom paid by God to the devil. It is interesting to note that Origen arrived at this theory in the capacity not of a dogmatic or constructive theologian but of an exegete. He was commenting on St Matthew's Gospel when he came to the words: " The Son of Man came not to be ministered unto, but to minister, and to give his life a ransom for many." [1] He asked himself, If Christ's life was a ransom, to whom was the ransom paid? He answered that man by his sin had sold his soul to the devil, and God had re-purchased man for himself by paying to the devil the ransom of Christ's life. This theory seems incredibly crude to us; and it is only fair to

[1] Matt. xx. 28 = Mark x. 45.

Origen to point out that this idea of ransom is only one of his many different cycles of ideas on the subject of redemption. Unlike Clement, he took the fact of redemption from sin seriously, and it is hardly too much to say that Origen hints at almost every way of approach to the question of the Atonement that has been put forward since his day. Clement's idea of Christian Gnosticism had led him to minimise the necessity of redemption ; for him salvation was from ignorance. But Origen recognises man's need of salvation, although he was a Christian Gnostic too ; he values the Christian doctrine of salvation by the Cross, but the crucifix is not for him the final expression of our religion : " Happy are they who no longer need the Saviour as Physician, Shepherd or Redemption, but as Wisdom, Word and Righteousness." [1]

Origen nowhere attempts to unify his various strands of thought on the subject of the Atonement. Nor does it ever occur to him that the Ransom Theory is unworthy of the Christian conception of God ; but over a century later Gregory of Nyssa (died A.D. 395), his follower in this matter, does attempt to answer the objection that the theory is an unworthy one. Gregory of Nyssa and Rufinus (c. A.D. 400) are the classic expositors of the Ransom Theory. What Origen leaves uncertain, Gregory makes quite clear. The devil did not perceive the Deity of Christ because it was veiled in his humanity, " so that, as with greedy fish, the hook of the Deity might be gulped

[1] *Cf.* Charles Bigg, *The Christian Platonists of Alexandria*, p. 171.

down along with the bait of the flesh." Christ, being divine, could not be conquered by death, and so the deceiver was by an act of strictly poetic justice deceived; in the infinite wisdom of God the devil was paid back in his own coin. Rufinus, in his *Commentary on the Apostles' Creed*, elaborates the metaphor of the bait and hook: Christ's flesh is the bait which lured the devil, his divinity is the hook on which he was caught. Gregory the Great (*c.* 540-604) varies the metaphor, suggesting the idea of a snare for birds. Perhaps the strangest form of the metaphor is found in Augustine, who likens the Cross to a mouse-trap baited with the blood of Christ. Thus it happened that Origen's passing suggestion came to enjoy extensive popularity; the Ransom Theory was the generally accepted view of the Atonement until the time of Anselm (died A.D. 1109). The last serious critic of the theory before Anselm's day was (curiously enough, since he was Gregory of Nyssa's great friend) Gregory of Nazianzum. The latter urged that the view was both unscriptural and unworthy of the character of God; he uses the strongest language concerning it, even going so far as to call it blasphemous.

The great Archbishop of Canterbury, Anselm, completely repudiated the Ransom Theory as unworthy of God; and he went on to build up with logical argument a new theory expressed in the terminology of his own day. In every age man thinks of God and his relation to the world in terms of contemporary social and political organisation; and in the Middle Ages God was naturally thought of as the supreme feudal Overlord, to whom all lesser beings owed allegiance and honour. Man owed honour to God as a squire or a serf might owe it to his feudal lord, or as a knight might owe it to his king. But by his sin man had dishonoured God, and he was powerless to render satisfaction for his disloyalty. In the days of chivalry it was possible to atone for an offence either by receiving the due punishment or by rendering "satisfaction," that is, by the restitution of the honour which had been outraged. God did not punish mankind because that would have meant the damnation of the whole human race; instead he found for man a way of rendering satisfaction so that the violated divine honour might be repaired. Man himself was unable to render satisfaction to God; therefore God in his mercy sent his Son who assumed manhood, and who, as man, rendered ample satisfaction by his innocent death. That is why God became man—so that man could thus render satisfaction for his disloyalty in the Person of Christ.[1] The debt of honour was paid for man by God incarnate in man; and thus God's violated honour was repaired, and God was able freely to forgive without the punishment of the guilty.

The " Satisfaction Theory " of Anselm's is obviously a great improvement upon the crude Ransom Theory. The devil as a possessor of rights is completely left out of the explanation, while on the other hand there is no suggestion of an angry God.

[1] *Cf.* the title of Anselm's treatise on the subject : *Cur Deus Homo ?*

The attractiveness of Anselm's theory for the medieval mind is shown by the fact that, although it was strikingly new, it won rapid and universal acceptance. It became the current view of the later Middle Ages, and the theologians of the Reformation built upon it, though it is doubtful whether they improved upon it. Its chief weakness is the weakness of all theories : it was the creature of its own times. Later ages could not regard God as a feudal Overlord after the days of chivalry had passed ; and the explanation of the Atonement in terms of " honour " and " satisfaction " was suitable only in the days when society was ordered upon a feudal basis. The conception of God as feudal Lord is not so universal as the conception of him as Father ; and the theory of Anselm tended to stress God's honour rather than his love.

We now come to our third type of theory, which is often called the Penal Theory, for reasons which will appear. The Renaissance brought with it a revival of interest in ancient law ; and we are consequently not surprised to find that the Reformation divines work out a theory of the Atonement in legal terms. The Penal Theory is grounded upon the new political and legal ideas of the sixteenth century ; it starts from the ideas of the inviolability of law and the justice of God. God is perfectly just, and the divine law of punishment can never be set aside. Man by his transgression has earned the dreadful punishment which the inviolable law of God must inflict. God's justice is such that sin cannot go unpunished. But the extent of man's sin is infinite: an infinitely severe punishment is its inevitable consequence. However, God is not only just, he is also merciful; and he himself in his infinite mercy provided a substitute who, being of an infinite nature, should be able to bear the punishment for the sins of the whole world. Thus, Christ came down to offer himself as our substitute; he bore the punishment instead of us; and by so doing he rendered it possible for God to forgive sins, and at the same time to remain perfect both in his justice and his mercy. It is sometimes objected against this theory that God is not thus shown to be just but rather unjust, in that he allows the innocent to suffer for the guilty; this, however, is not a valid objection to the theory as stated by the Reformation divines: for the latter, dwelling on the Pauline saying that the sinless Christ "was made to be sin for us,"[1] did not hesitate to assert that Christ so completely identified himself with mankind that he was also identified with sin: Christ is a sinner himself. Thus Luther says: "This saw all the prophets, that Christ was to be of all men the greatest robber, murderer, thief, profaner, blasphemer, and so on . . . who bears in his own body all the sins of men—not in that he committed them, but in that he took upon his own body the things committed by us, to make satisfaction for them with his own blood."[2]

Of course, the Penal Theory seems to us crude

[1] 2 Cor. v. 21.
[2] Quoted by Professor L. W. Grensted, *History of the Doctrine of the Atonement*, p. 200.

and repellent. But it was natural that society at a certain stage of its evolution should believe that its laws are so sacred that every violation of them must receive plenary punishment. Nowadays we hold very different ideas about the ethics of punishment. In modern society justice does not mean merely the infliction of punishment after transgression: the society which inexorably carries out this penalty is not necessarily thought by us to be ideally just. We cannot believe that God must find "satisfaction" in punishment before he can forgive: not so does an earthly father treat his children's offences. To such a criticism the supporters of the Satisfaction type of theory might reply that, after all, God cannot act just as a private individual, since he has a universe to run; he has to maintain discipline, check corruption and administer justice; it is necessary for the orderly running of the world that the strict principles of justice be maintained. To which line of argument we can only answer that we must choose which picture of God seems to us most adequate, the picture of God as Judge or the picture of him as Father; but we may claim with some confidence the authority of Jesus for the latter. In Jesus' great parable of atonement the father of the Prodigal Son did not wait for the laws of justice to do their work: he went out to meet him while he was yet a long way off. It is perhaps not too presumptuous a claim to make that our social and ethical ideas have evolved a long way since the sixteenth century; and consequently we cannot rest content with the Reformation theories of the

Atonement.   Many men and women of our own
generation have been repelled from Christianity by
old-fashioned teachers insisting upon some form
of the Penal Theory ; but it is these people who
have rebelled against the inadequate ethical con-
ceptions of an earlier age, rather than their teachers,
whose outlook is the more Christian : they are
the men and women who, through false teaching
given in Christ's name, have denied Christ for
Christ's sake.

Very few people nowadays feel satisfied with any
of the theories of the Atonement which we have
so far discussed, and it is a real consolation to reflect
that none of these theories can claim to be binding
upon Christians.   There is another theory, often
called the Moral Theory, which makes a greater
appeal to the modern mind, although it is by no
means a modern invention.   It is usually associated
with the name of Abelard (1079-1142), who criti-
cised and rejected Anselm's Satisfaction Theory as
well as the Ransom Theory ; but it is a mistake
to look upon Abelard as the only champion of
the theory until comparatively recent times.   The
Moral Theory has often been hinted at since the
days of the Greek Fathers.   The uniqueness of the
case of Abelard lies rather in the fact that he is
the only outstanding example of a thinker who
has been condemned because of his individualistic
view of the Atonement.   Abelard held that the
Cross is the most appealing exhibition of God's
love : the appeal of suffering love—of Jesus
crucified by man's folly, pride and sin—converts
the sinner as no other appeal could ever do.

The Moral Theory thus suggests that men are saved by the appeal of Christ's self-giving love : in looking upon Christ's death we see the love of God made manifest, and thus we are ashamed of our own selfishness and blindness, and we come to seek amendment of life and to accept the free gift of God's love. The Cross, therefore, brings repentance to men, because it shows more clearly than anything else has ever done the suffering inflicted by human callousness and pride upon the Father's love. Calvary is thus the school of penitence of the human race, for there men of all ages and races have learned the depth and power of the love of God. Jesus finally brought home to men by his death what he had never quite succeeded in imparting by his teaching, that the greatest thing in life is self-giving love, and that true greatness consists in the ability to become the servant of all. The Cross has been the most powerful moral influence in history, bringing to men that repentance which renders them able to be forgiven. For God always desires to forgive, but cannot forgive until men repent and seek amendment of life. Thus God in Christ saves the world from sin and its consequence, spiritual death ; he makes forgiveness possible and liberates men to a life of service and true happiness. He reconciles the world unto himself.

This theory has found many supporters in modern times, though it was frequently (and perhaps unconsciously) held by ancient and medieval thinkers alongside of their other views. Its strength lies in its simplicity, its freedom from crude ideas of ransom, satisfaction, and so on, and in the fact that it casts no unfavourable shadow upon the character of God. It represents God as Father, not as devil's Deceiver, feudal Overlord or Judge. Its weakness, as its critics urge, lies in the fact that it makes salvation dependent upon what man does (that is, upon his own efforts after repentance and amendment) as much as upon what God does : man saves himself by looking upon the Crucified. The extent to which reconciliation is achieved depends ultimately upon what men do, upon their conversion or repentance ; and thus, in the long run, God's attitude towards mankind— whether he is able to forgive them or not—depends upon their attitude towards Jesus. The theory stresses the *Christus Crucifixus* rather than the *Christus Victor* of the ancient classical formulations ; it points to the patheric, mute appeal of the Crucified —" Is it nothing to you, all ye who pass by ? "— rather than to the victory which God has gloriously won for man. Such criticism is to some extent justified : the Moral Theory is very helpful and true so far as it goes, but it is not the whole truth : it does not explain all that the Christian experience of forgiveness contains. It does not explain our experience of *Christus Regnans*.

Dr Gustaf Aulén has pleaded for a return to the ancient conception of Christ as King. He redirects our attention to what God has achieved for man by Christ's victory over sin. Modern people might interpret this thought in some such way as the following : As Christians we share our Lord's belief that the only omnipotent force in the world

is love. Love's purpose, we believe, cannot fail,
since love is the ultimate law and nature of reality.
God's purpose of love will finally triumph: it
cannot for ever be thwarted by the human misuse
of free will. The eternal victory of love is assured,
is, in fact, already won. This is what we mean
when we talk of Christ's conquest of sin, death
and the devil. Sin is not invincible: God can
ultimately achieve the conversion of every human
soul: death and sin shall not defeat his purpose.
We shall therefore probably be led to reject a
view which at the present time has won a certain
measure of support, the view that only those who
repent and prove themselves worthy of eternal life
shall gain it (a view which the Moral Theory
encourages), while the rest of mankind who have
rejected God's way shall be annihilated altogether.
This view is sometimes known as the doctrine of
Conditional Immortality, and it seems to provide
for some modern preachers a convenient substitute
for the now unfashionable doctrine of hell-fire.
Such a view implies that God's purpose of love
must to some extent fail, since a certain percentage
of the human race must be extinguished altogether;
love is thus not strictly omnipotent. Christ has
only partially triumphed over sin and death. As
against such a doctrine we must insist that Christ
has completely vanquished sin and death, or, in
other words, that God's purpose must succeed in
respect of every created soul. And what God's
purpose of love has eternally secured, Christ's victory on the human level has in the world of time
permanently assured. Christ's victory in time is

the sign and symbol of God's eternal victory, just as his wooden cross on Calvary is the symbol in time of God's eternal nature of love.

Let us summarise our argument thus : Historical Christianity is committed to the principle—inherent in Christian experience—that through Jesus Christ God has won for men salvation from sin and eternal life. But historical Christianity commits us to no one theory of the Atonement. We are free to construct our own theory of how Christ saves men, that is, we are free to attempt to explain it to ourselves. But we must, of course, see to it that we do not explain away the principle grounded upon the experience of forgiveness in Christ. We have suggested that if we combine the Moral Theory with the old classical Christian view summed up in the phrase *Christus Victor*, we shall arrive at a tolerably satisfactory explanation in terms acceptable to the modern mind. Our explanation must somehow account for the paradox inherent in the Christian experience—that the *Christus Crucifixus* is the *Christus Regnans*. Christ's victory is the victory of suffering love, and it is our assurance of the final success of God's plan for the world ; men appropriate to themselves the fruits of Christ's victory by the repentance which he renders possible. Christ's victory is complete : God's purpose cannot fail : Christ's triumph is the expression and assurance in time of the eternal consummation.

Some such explanation as this seems to be involved in the classical, Scriptural and credal formulations of the Christian faith as well as in the Christian experience of redemption itself. But our purpose all along has been to set before the reader the main facts of the historical development of Christian doctrines rather than to inculcate any special theory.   Each must interpret as he is able. Everyone must seek his own explanation which his own experience and that of the whole Church suggest.   Moreover, we must remember that the experience is primary, while the theory is only secondary.   Throughout all our discussions we must not forget that theory should be but an aid to practice, and that there is an art as well as a theory of Atonement.   Those who practise the art are best qualified to understand the theory, for Christian doctrines and theories about them are not abstract things removed altogether from real life.   " If any man willeth to do his will, he shall know of the doctrine." [1]

[1] John vii. 17.

CHAPTER VI

THE DOCTRINE OF THE HOLY SPIRIT

IN several earlier passages, especially in the chapter in which we considered the doctrine of the Trinity, we have already touched upon the Person and work of the Holy Spirit. But for the sake of completeness, and since the doctrine of the Holy Spirit puzzles so many people to-day, it is perhaps desirable to discuss this doctrine somewhat more fully in this concluding chapter.

Christianity inherited from Judaism the conception of a living, active God, who was the controller of the fortunes of individual men and women as well as of the destinies of nations. In Greek religion, as we have noticed above, the Supreme God was relegated to a realm of heavenly bliss far removed from the changes and chances of mundane life ; it was not he who was active in human affairs, but a hierarchy of lesser gods and demi-gods. The great advantage of the Jewish over the Greek view was that, for the former, the action of God in the world was co-ordinated towards definite moral ends : it was unified and consistent; but, on the Greek view, the divine activity in our world was chaotic, conflicting and capricious : the gods and demi-gods did not always pull in the same direction. The Christian religion in its beginnings owed a great deal to Judaism and practically nothing to

Greek religion. The Christians conceived of God as ever-present and ever-active in the world; but whereas the Jews had tended to limit Jehovah's activity to the fortunes of his Chosen Race, Christianity realised that the activity of God extended over the whole range of human life in every time and place. Primitive Christianity believed profoundly in the ceaseless activity of God in the world, and this belief is the raw material, as it were, of the Church's doctrine of the Holy Spirit. For that doctrine, like every other great doctrine of historical Christianity, is grounded upon experience; the early Christians, who after the resurrection carried the good news all over the Empire, experienced the continued inspiration of the presence of God, leading, guiding, encouraging and sustaining them. The literature of the early Church, for example, the Book of Acts or the Epistles of St Paul, speaks continually of this experience of divine leadership and inspiration which the earliest missionaries enjoyed. Wherever they went they felt the presence and power of God.

This God of their own direct experiencing was mediated by Jesus, their Risen Lord, whose Spirit now filled the world. Their experience of God was always for them a living communion with the Master who had led them from Galilee to Jerusalem. We may put this in another way by saying that their religious experience was, as it were, flavoured with the personality of the historical Jesus whom the original disciples had known in his earthly life. God was now seen to possess the character and quality of Jesus. The great Spirit of the world, hitherto ignorantly worshipped by genuinely religious pagans as Logos, or the pervading Reason of God, now received a name; the immanent Spirit recognised by Greek philosophers and men of religion was discovered to be the Spirit of Jesus—as he had been known in Galilee—on a cosmic scale. The Unknown God was now felt to possess a character, the character of the love that was in Jesus Christ. The early Christians found that the Spirit of their Master so completely filled the world that they at once came to identify the immanent Spirit of God in the universe with the now universalised Spirit of their Risen Lord.

Thus it happens that in the New Testament we find the phrases " Spirit of God " and " Spirit of Jesus " used more or less interchangeably. The immanent Spirit, which was the object of religious experience, was the Spirit both of God and of Christ. The functions attributed to the Holy Spirit in the New Testament are those attributed to Jehovah in the Old : it is the Spirit who leads, guides, sanctifies, assists in prayer, inspires and builds up the body of the Church. Though the Holy Spirit is never in the New Testament explicitly called God, there can be no doubt that he was regarded by the New Testament writers as divine, because all these functions are so obviously the work of God alone. Moreover, they are also personal : the Holy Spirit is equally obviously regarded as a person by the writers of the New Testament.

But the New Testament writers are not systematic theologians; they do not attempt to define the exact relationship of the Holy Spirit to the Father or the Risen Christ. There is no clear demarcation of language. Sometimes it is the Father, sometimes the Risen Lord, sometimes the Holy Spirit, who is said to be the source of a certain gift or operation. This clearly implies that the New Testament writers hold fast to the Jewish conception of the unity of the Godhead; there is distinction in the Godhead, but it is a distinction within unity. There is no hint in the New Testament of a doctrine of Three Gods. What is implied is a doctrine of one God, revealed as Father, Son and Holy Spirit. But the Holy Spirit is not a personality distinct from the personality of God; he is rather God in action, God at work in the world. By the New Testament writers God is thought of as Father in relation to his work of creation: he is the Lord of the Universe and Source of all Being; he is thought of as Son in relation to his work of self-revelation through his incarnation in the historical person of Jesus Christ; he is thought of as Spirit in relation to his gifts of love, joy, peace, grace, prophecy, ministry, healing, and so on, or, more briefly, in relation to his work of sanctification. But it is the one God who creates, redeems and sanctifies.

Thus the Holy Spirit in the New Testament is God in action in the lives of men. He is God, sanctifying, inspiring and enabling mankind. The subsequent doctrine of the Holy Spirit as developed by the Church after the close of the apostolic period loyally conserves the teaching of the New Testament. It introduces nothing for which sanction cannot be found in the New Testament. It only makes explicit what is implicit in the New Testament literature. For instance, although the Spirit is not actually called God in the New Testament, yet the implicit belief in his divinity is undeniable ; it was natural, therefore, that the Church should go on explicitly to confess the Godhead of the Spirit. But this explicit recognition of the divinity of the Spirit did not take place for some time ; the evolution of the Church's theology was a slow process, and when at length formulations were seen to be necessary, they were drawn up primarily with a view to the refutation of heretical teaching. The Church was not anxious to claim a complete knowledge of the inner nature and counsels of God ; for her own part she was content with the revelation of God's character and purpose contained in the New Testament, but the heretics compelled her to defend the New Testament faith by suggesting theories which would ultimately have destroyed it.

It was the teaching of the later Arians of the second half of the fourth century which called forth the strongest assertion of the divinity of the Holy Spirit which had yet been put forward. They said that the Holy Spirit was a creature, just as the angels or ministering spirits were creatures, or just as the earlier Arians had argued that Christ was only a creature. Hence, in the so-called Nicene Creed (which, as we have seen earlier, was really the Creed adopted by the Council of Constantinople in the year 381), which may be found in the Church of England Communion Service, we find these words as they appear in the original version:

> " We believe in the Holy Spirit, the Lord and Giver of life, who proceedeth from the Father, who with the Father and the Son together is worshipped and glorified, who spake by the prophets."

We may note that in this important confession of the Church's faith the Holy Spirit is still not explicitly called God, although it contains a weighty statement that the Son is " very God of very God." This illustrates the conservative nature of the early formularies, and reminds us that in the fourth century conservative theologians of irreproachable orthodoxy still hesitated to use language which was not actually the language of the New Testament and the primitive Church. Nevertheless, as we pointed out above,[1] this passage definitely implies belief in the full Godhead of the Holy Spirit, for (with the Second Commandment in mind) it was sternly forbidden to worship anything other than God. If the Spirit was to be " worshipped and glorified " together with the Father and the Son, the Spirit must be fully divine. The Church had indeed all along " worshipped and glorified " the Spirit together with the Father and the Son. For example, an ancient hymn which probably dates from the second century, the *Gloria in Excelsis Deo* (which may be found at the end

---

[1] See p. 56 above.

of the Communion Service in the Book of Common
Prayer), explicitly says that the Holy Spirit is
worthy of worship and praise together with the
Father and the Son :

"For thou only art holy ; thou only art the
Lord ; thou only, O Christ, with the Holy
Spirit, art most high in the glory of God the
Father."

In this way the primitive Church had always
linked the worship of the Spirit with that of the
Father and the Son.   This is the clearest proof
of the recognition of the divinity of the Spirit
from the earliest times, for the *lex credendi* is one
with the *lex orandi*—the Church's worship is always
based upon the Church's belief.

The explicit statement of the Church's faith in
the divinity of the Spirit is made without quali-
fication in the fifth century.   Thus, the Definition
put forward by the Fathers at Chalcedon quotes
the so-called Nicene Creed (*i.e.* the Creed ratified
by the Council of Constantinople in 381), and adds
that the clauses concerning the Holy Spirit were
inserted for the following reason :

"On account of those who fight against the
Holy Spirit, it (the Council of Chalcedon) rati-
fies the teaching handed down at a later date
(*i.e.* 381) by the one hundred and fifty Holy
Fathers assembled in the Imperial City (*i.e.*
Constantinople, now the capital of the Eastern
Empire) concerning the essence of the Spirit ;
which teaching they made known to all, not

as adducing anything left lacking by their predecessors (*i.e.* the Bishops at Nicea in 325), but making clear by means of Scriptural testimonies their conception of the Holy Spirit against those who were trying to set aside his Sovereignty."

Similarly, the *Quicunque Vult* (the so-called Athanasian Creed), which almost certainly dates from towards or about the middle of the fifth century, definitely states that :

" The Father is God ; the Son is God ; and the Holy Spirit is God. And yet they are not three Gods, but one God."

In this Creed the Trinitarian position is explicitly stated, as we noted in Chapter III ; the Holy Spirit is said to be equal to the Father in divinity, majesty, quality and power. God is to be worshipped as Trinity in Unity, Unity in Trinity. Thus the belief in the divinity of the Holy Spirit which we find implicit in the New Testament is made explicit in the later formulations of the Church's faith.

In a similar way the New Testament belief in the personal nature of the Holy Spirit was preserved in the later doctrine of the Church. At first there was a good deal of uncertainty as to the nature of the Spirit ; we find that even in the New Testament itself there is a tendency to drop the definite article in the phrase " the Holy Spirit." This usage might lend colour to the crude view that the Spirit is a commodity rather than a person: the Greek Testament (mainly in the writings of St Luke) several times uses the phrase "filled with Holy Spirit."[1] Down to the fourth century there were some who regarded the Spirit as an energy, a principle or a commodity, rather than as a person. But those who held such views do not seem to have been either numerous or influential; the majority of the Fathers regarded the Holy Spirit (as we have seen that the New Testament does) as a person with whom we may enter into definitely personal relations, and whose work is in the fullest sense personal.

In our chapter on the Trinity (Chapter III) we have already discussed the relation of the Holy Spirit to the Father and the Son. It is not necessary here to repeat our caution that the ancient use of the word "person" (as it is found in the classical formulations of the Christian faith) differs considerably from its modern meaning of "personality." We need here only remind ourselves that the Holy Spirit was not generally held by the ancient Church to have a personality distinct from the personality of God.[2] The Spirit is not to be conceived of as a second personality (in the modern sense) over against the personality of God. He is rather God himself in action—God immanent in the world.

Thus the doctrine of the Holy Spirit is a doctrine of God's immanence; it implies that God, at work

[1] *Cf.* Luke i. 41, 67; Acts iv. 8; ix. 17; xiii. 9; but see also Eph. v. 18.

[2] *Cf.* Swete, *Holy Spirit in the Ancient Church*, pp. 375 f., quoted above, p. 65

in the world, is not to be conceived of as a mere impersonal agency, a principle of evolution, a "life-force," or a tendency in the nature of things towards progress. The Christian doctrine of God is, by its traditional belief in the Holy Spirit, utterly removed from those modern philosophies which admit deity only in the sense of an impersonal force at work in the nature of things. God is a Being with whom we may enter into personal relationships and who possesses a character as clearly defined as that of Jesus Christ. He is no vague, abstract Absolute or Force which moves blindly, a God who (like Bergson's or Alexander's) walks in his sleep; he is the active, living God of Old as well as New Testament experience—a God who neither slumbers nor sleeps. The Church's doctrine of the Holy Spirit implies that God is not less than personal, that he is in the fullest sense conscious, and that he has a purpose for the world.

The Church teaches that the Spirit which fills the world, inspiring, encouraging and enabling, is, as it were, the Spirit of the Supreme God. It is not that the Spirit is a mediator between man and the Supreme God, for the Spirit is the Spirit of the Supreme God, is God immanent, is indeed God himself. This is what is meant by the theological formula which says that the Holy Spirit "proceeds" from the Father. In theological language, God the Father is the Source of Godhead and indeed of all being; he "generates" the Son, and the Holy Spirit "proceeds" from him. In technical language it is correct to speak

of the " generation " of the Son and of the " procession " of the Spirit ; but we need not be afraid
of these ancient usages, since they mean only that
the revelation of God in Jesus Christ and by the
works of the Spirit manifest in our world is a
revelation of the Supreme God, the Creator of
this vast universe himself; they are of God and
from God and in God. In the West it became
customary to say that the Holy Spirit proceeds
from the Father and the Son, because it was felt
that the Spirit, though proceeding ultimately from
the Father as the Source of all being, was given
to the world by Jesus Christ, and because the New
Testament speaks of him as the Spirit of Jesus as
well as the Spirit of the Father. But the Eastern
Church never accepted this usage, although it was
mainly a matter of words and terminology, no
vital theological issue being involved ; and so,
after considerable controversy, about the eighth
century, the matter became a pretext for the final
severance of the Western and Eastern Churches in
the Middle Ages, when relations between the two
Churches were severely strained and the true sense
of Christian unity had been obscured. The Eastern
Church was right in that the " *Filioque* Clause "
(the addition of the words " and the Son " after
the words " who proceedeth from the Father ")
was not part of the Nicene Creed accepted at
Constantinople in the year 381 ; but the Western
Church was right in urging that the doctrine of
the " Double Procession " (*i.e.* the doctrine that
the Spirit proceeds from the Father and the Son)
was at least as old as Tertullian (*c.* A.D. 200), who

held that the Spirit proceeds from the Father *through* the Son—which was, of course, all that the Western Church implied by the doctrine. To modern people the disagreement will seem trivial and merely verbal; and so indeed it largely is. When the sense of Christian unity is lost, however, any pretext will serve as an excuse for a breaking of the fellowship.

The Church to-day sorely needs to reawaken to the full realisation of the significance of her ancient doctrine of God as Holy Spirit. Only by so doing will she be able to overcome the devitalising and ancient superstition that God is remote and uninterested in the affairs of men—a position to which we all too easily revert when we lose touch with the Christian experience of the Holy Spirit. She must renew in this present age her fellowship with the active, living God, whose leadership and creative work in the world to-day is no less real and powerful than in the pioneer days of Paul's first Gentile mission. For this is the practical meaning of the doctrine of the Holy Spirit: God is still to-day at work in the world, as Revealer, Restorer and Redeemer. The reality of the experience of God in the world is discoverable only by those who will co-operate with God and allow his Spirit to use them for his creative work. It is those who themselves have been carried along by the dynamic energy of the Spirit of God in the quest for the great ideals of truth, beauty and righteousness who are best qualified to witness to the power of the Holy Spirit, just as in the first century it was to the adventurers who carried

the good news of the resurrection that the first
revelation of God as Holy Spirit was made.

The experience of the Holy Spirit is not re-
stricted to priests or theologians, or to any caste or
sect ; it may be enjoyed by all men in every sphere
of life. Christians believe that every aspiration
towards social righteousness, every creative artistic
impulse, every scientific quest for truth, is a movement of God's Spirit in the world. For the Spirit
of God works in all whose lives are dedicated to
a noble ideal—in artists, scientists, reformers,
craftsmen and all honest workmen—whether with
their outward lips they profess and call themselves
Christians or not. We cannot forbid them because they follow not us, though we regret that
the fulness and joy of the wholly Christian life is
not theirs ; yet we rejoice that they too are being
used as instruments of the Spirit. The Christian
sees God's Spirit at work in every effort at international understanding or class co-operation. He
sees the Spirit at work filling the world with a
divine discontent with things as they are, and
hence, even in the chaos of the post-war world,
he is able to discern the operations of the Lord
and Giver of life. To this extent the Christian is
optimistic : because he believes in the Holy Spirit,
he has faith in the power of God to redeem and
sanctify all human relationships.

Too often has the ecclesiastical mind attempted
to confine the workings of the Spirit within the
narrow walls of denominational Christianity. But
it is a great mistake thus to set a limit to the
sphere of operation of the Spirit which bloweth

where it listeth. Nevertheless the Christian Church is, or should be, the true home of God's Spirit on the earth, or, to vary the metaphor, the supreme instrument of his activity in the world. The Spirit assuredly uses other instruments—the League of Nations, a Disarmament Conference or a Slum Clearance Committee, perhaps—but ideally, at any rate, the Church is his instrument *par excellence*. That is her sole *raison d'être*. For the Church is still the living body of Christ on earth, his incarnation in the twentieth century, and through the Church the Spirit moves towards the sanctification of the world. The Church, the Christian community, ought to be a city set on a hill, the leaven which leavens the lump, the antiseptic of society.

The Christian religion has always taught that the work of the Spirit is that of sanctification. To sanctify means to make holy, that is, to purge of sin and selfishness and to liberate for the service of God. Historical Christianity teaches that God in Christ has already achieved the world's redemption (as we saw in the last chapter), and that the Holy Spirit carries on the work of sanctification, that is, of leading men to appropriate to themselves the fruits of that redemption. This is God's work in the world, the function of the Holy Spirit : to offer to men the riches of God, made available for our race by Jesus Christ, and thus to redeem and sanctify all human relationships, till the consummation of God's eternal purpose be achieved.

This means the creation of a new world, a

world peopled by redeemed men and women, living consequently in a sanctified social order, a world in which all things are made new and in which we are given all those good things for which we long, but which, save by the grace of God, we are powerless to attain. This vision of the goal towards which the Spirit of God tirelessly leads mankind is the blessing which he offers to us through the prophets of our race and by which he encourages us to renewed effort towards fuller co-operation with him. It is this vision which inspires and animates what would otherwise be the dry bones of the Church's theology ; for Christian doctrine is merely the vessel in which the inspiration has been conveyed : it is now our task to purvey it in new vessels to our own perplexed and groping generation. Yet it is not a new vision, but a vision which the prophets of our race have seen since long before the day when the light shone clear from Galilee. This vision of a new world, which has fascinated men since the days when the searching gaze of the Hebrew prophets first looked beyond their nationalistic horizons by the miracle of the Spirit's inspiration, has never received nobler expression than in the words of a prophet whose very name has been forgotten and whose writings have been given to the world under the name of another. Upon these burning words Jesus himself pondered in the workshop of Nazareth, until the day came when he took it as the charter of his own life's mission at the outset of his ministry of preaching.[1]

[1] Luke iv. 17-19.

It is a vision which indwells the Church's theology of the Holy Spirit and sets forth in haunting language her conception of the purpose of God:

> " The Spirit of the Lord God is upon me; because the Lord hath anointed me to preach good tidings unto the meek; he hath sent me to bind up the broken-hearted, to proclaim liberty to the captives, and the opening of the prison to them that are bound; to proclaim the acceptable year of the Lord, and the day of vengeance of our God: to comfort all that mourn; to appoint unto them that mourn in Zion, to give them beauty for ashes, the oil of joy for mourning, the garment of praise for the spirit of heaviness; that they might be called trees of righteousness, the planting of the Lord, that he might be glorified.   And they shall build the old wastes, they shall raise up the former desolations, and they shall repair the waste cities, the desolations of many generations." [1]

To such a programme is committed everyone who believes in the Church's doctrine of the Holy Spirit, and with such a vision is he blessed. Possessed of this commission and this blessing, he will endeavour to understand the deepest meaning of the Church's theology. To such a one that theology will no longer appear a barren wilderness of formulæ but an inexhaustible fountain of wisdom; and the historical doctrines of the

[1] Is. lxi. 1-4.

Church will cease to be dry and empty vessels, but will become an abiding well of living water, replenishing the springs of devotion and resolve. For at the bottom of the well is the truth which sets men free—free to understand, free to love, and free to serve.